Jossey-Bass Teacher

Jossey-Bass Teacher provides educators with practical knowledge and tools to create a positive and lifelong impact on student learning. We offer classroom-tested and research-based teaching resources for a variety of grade levels and subject areas. Whether you are an aspiring, new, or veteran teacher, we want to help you make every teaching day your best.

From ready-to-use classroom activities to the latest teaching framework, our value-packed books provide insightful, practical, and comprehensive materials on the topics that matter most to K–12 teachers. We hope to become your trusted source for the best ideas from the most experienced and respected experts in the field.

Praise for Phonics Pathways 10th Edition
By Dolores Hiskes

"*Phonics Pathways* is a classic proven solution to eliminate illiteracy in America. It provides teachers and parents with the tools to teach anyone to read fluently and proficiently. Dolores has captured the essence of effective, timeless teaching techniques with humor and precision, and put them into one simple to use, inexpensive manual. Every teacher of reading should have one."

> —**Robert W. Sweet, Jr.,** *president, The National Right to Read*
> *Foundation, former Reagan White House policy staffer,*
> *former senior staff member, U.S. House of Representatives,*
> *Committee on Education and the Workforce*

"*Phonics Pathways* was crucial in teaching my eighth grade remedial reading class. The book worked beautifully with a full class of 31 students. The class moved from 48% of students reading far below basic to 13%. Below basic scores started at 44% to climb to 52% reading at the basic level on district administered tests."

> —**Tasia James,** *CORE teacher,*
> *Christensen Middle School, Livermore, California*

"*Phonics Pathways* is the best book on the market for parents, teachers, or tutors who want to teach early reading skills. It provides research-based, explicit, systematic phonics and multi-syllable instruction in easy, self-guided lessons."

> —**Catherine Froggatt,** *R.N., Michigan State Director,*
> *The National Right to Read Foundation*

"I've used *Phonics Pathways* with my struggling readers for years, and absolutely LOVE how well it has helped them learn to read with confidence. Now with the expanded section on dividing multi-syllable words, I finally have a way to teach reading multi-syllable words to ALL my students. I also love the addition of the pictures to illustrate every sound."

> —**Trisha Sluder,** *second grade teacher,*
> *Murrieta Valley Unified School District*

"*Phonics Pathways* is a wonderful teaching tool! Every kindergarten and first grade teacher should have a copy in their hands. If this were the case, intervention in the grades that follow would be a thing of the past. Just like *Phonics Pathways,* I strongly recommend that teachers use *Phonics Pathways Boosters* during Workshop or Universal Access. Regular use of *Phonics Pathways* and *Phonics Pathways Boosters* will definitely boost your students reading scores!"

> —**Pamela M. Barret,** *instructional coach and consultant*

"I am trained in dyslexia and have used numerous programs to help students diagnosed with dyslexia, but nothing I have used, regardless of the price or sophistication, has come even close to *Phonics Pathways* for speed and efficiency of remediation. Students who begin learning to read with *Phonics Pathways* will never experience any problem with reading or spelling."

—Donald Potter,
experienced reading teacher and internet publisher

"We particularly like the *Phonics Pathways* program. For the average—and certainly the new—homeschooling parent, I enjoy the simplicity, yet completeness, of *Phonics Pathways*. Everything you need is included in the book. Instructions are concise, clear, and free of professional vocabulary. It's one of our favorite books!"

—Jessie Wise *and* **Susan Wise Bauer,** *authors of*
The Well-Trained Mind: A Guide to Classical Education At Home

"Our two adopted seven-year-old sons are learning disabled, and one of them has ADD as well. He is repeating his SLD second grade class. After only two months of *Phonics Pathways* he is reading at the upper level of grade three—it's a miracle!

"My son's speech pathologist is now using it with her fourteen-year-old student, and three other teachers are waiting to get their copy. The wealth of word lists, spelling rules, blending exercises, and practice sentences make it a rich resource that would enhance any reading program.

"When I finally had to return my library copy the woman standing in back of me put it on reserve for herself. If everyone knew how easy and fast this book works and how inexpensive it is, it would put the more expensive programs right out of business."

—Bonnie Miller, *mom, Greenacres, Florida*

"Our elementary instructors are in-serviced in the use of *Phonics Pathways*. They have experienced great success in using it with a wide variety of students: English as a Second Language, remedial, beginning reading, dyslexic, and even adults.

"It is clear and well organized, and has large print. The skills are sequenced correctly, the sketches humorous, the proverbs encouraging, and the hints very useful. Combining reading and spelling and applying the skill in words and sentences is most helpful.

"This outstanding resource has helped many students learn to read and spell, and given teachers confidence in teaching phonics, spelling, and reading. I highly recommend it for all students who are learning to read."

—Christine Knight, *faculty facilitator, Schoolcraft College, Michigan*

"I am a special ed teacher at a Day Treatment program. These are the kids no school knows how to handle anymore but are not severe enough to go into a residential program. Half my kids have severe learning problems leading to behavioral problems, and half have severe behavioral problems leading to learning problems.

I tried *Phonics Pathways*, and the results are really good! My fourth and fifth graders who read at a kindergarten level before we started now can read many words after only 18 lessons. The blending exercises taught them how to decode words, and they now automatically use the same strategies to decode new and long words.

The parents of these kids think I am some kind of genius because finally I got their kids to read. And it's so beautiful and rewarding to see their self esteem grow also—this is what makes teaching so rewarding. Thank you sooo much for your book!

—**Renee Wesly,** *special ed teacher,*
Maunawili Elementary School, Kailua, Hawaii

"I started *Phonics Pathways* in K3, the last year of kindergarten in Taiwan. After only four months these six- and seven-year-olds began reading story books and never looked back! K3 has surpassed my wildest dreams, as they read far better than any other class at school. They put students who've studied for up to six years to shame.

"One mother told me her daughter reads her e-mail, and although it has a lot of technical terms her daughter reads it better than she does. And she has a college degree! Parents are amazed that their little ones can read at such an early age, even before they are quite at ease with Chinese characters.

"A funny story: I was substitute teaching an older class that had been learning English for at least six years. When I told them K3 could read better and more fluent than they could they laughed and didn't believe me. Just then, Sunny, a K3 student passed, and I called her in. We held a reading contest, and little Sunny beat the whole class!"

—**Rudi Kerkhoffs,** *kindergarten and first grade teacher, Taiwan*

Phonics Pathways

Clear Steps to Easy Reading and Perfect Spelling, 10th Edition

Dolores G. Hiskes

JOSSEY-BASS
A Wiley Imprint
www.josseybass.com

Published by Jossey-Bass
A Wiley Imprint
989 Market Street, San Francisco, CA 94103-1741   www.josseybass.com

Jossey-Bass books and products are available through most bookstores. To contact Jossey-Bass directly call our Customer Care Department within the U.S. at 800-956-7739, outside the U.S. at 317-572-3986, or fax 317-572-4002.

Jossey-Bass also publishes its books in a variety of electronic formats. Some content that appears in print may not be available in electronic books.

ISBN 978-1-118-02243-6 (paper)
ISBN 978-1-118-03721-8 (ebook)
ISBN 978-1-118-03720-1 (ebook)
ISBN 978-1-118-03719-5 (ebook)

Printed in the United States of America

TENTH EDITION

PB Printing 10 9 8 7 6 5 4

About This Book

With the use of a clever icon, Dewey the Bookworm, *Phonics Pathways* teaches students of all ages the rudiments of phonics and spelling with an efficient, practical, and foolproof method.

Phonics Pathways is organized by sounds and spelling patterns. They are introduced one at a time, and slowly built into words, syllables, phrases, and sentences. Simple step-by-step directions begin every lesson. Extensive examples, word lists, and practice readings are 100 percent decodable.

Each new step builds upon previously learned skills for continuous review and reinforcement. Learning in small, incremental steps is easier for everyone, especially students with learning disabilities or very short attention spans.

A multisensory method is used to address all learning styles, and every letter introduced is illustrated with multiple pictures beginning with its sound. These features are especially helpful to second-language students.

Although most appropriate for K–2 emergent readers, this award-winning book also is successfully being used with adolescent and adult learners, as well as second-language learners and students with learning disabilities.

Perfect both for schools and for use at home, this text offers specific strategies for dyslexic readers as well as beginners. Wise, humorous proverbs encourage virtues such as patience, perseverance, honesty, kindness, compassion, courage, and loyalty.

Contents

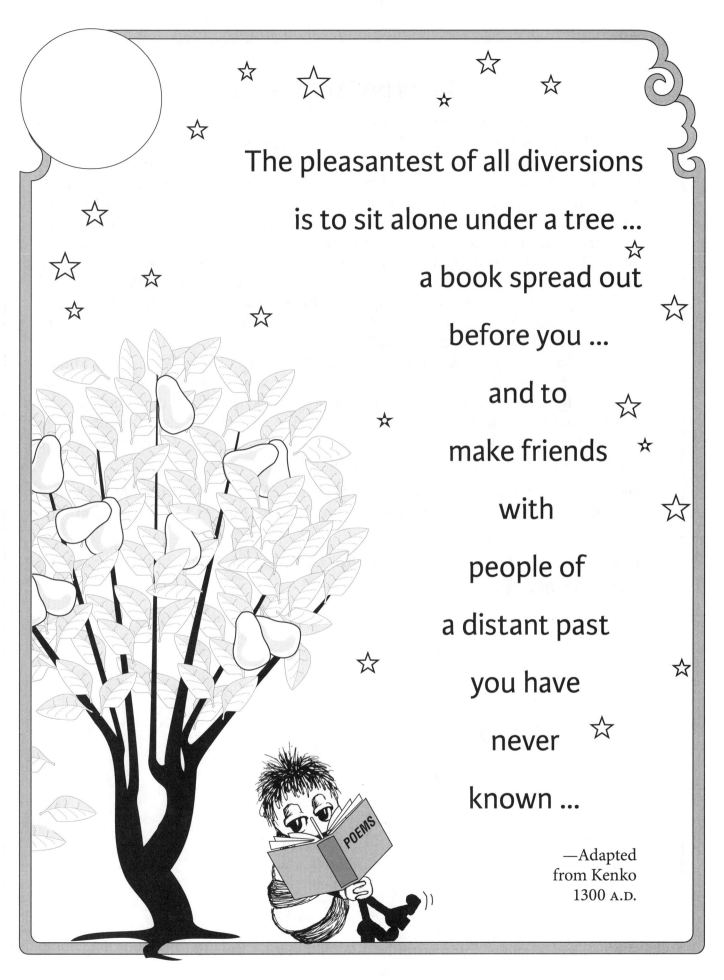

The pleasantest of all diversions

is to sit alone under a tree ...

a book spread out

before you ...

and to

make friends

with

people of

a distant past

you have

never

known ...

—Adapted
from Kenko
1300 A.D.

Acknowledgments

I will always and forever be grateful to: our beloved children Robin and Grant, who inspired a passion for teaching reading in the very beginning … our sweet young grandchildren Connor and Austen, who rekindled this passion … my eternal love and gratitude to my dearly-beloved best friend Johnny: a shiny gold medal for his love, support, and invaluable (if blunt) critiques, and a big purple heart for his valiant battles with insomnia while pretending to sleep through the never-ending 4:00 a.m. clicking, whirring, and whining of the computer and laser printer in our bedroom … Bob and Joy Sweet of the National Right To Read Foundation for their support, warm friendship, and encouragement since the very beginning … our treasured friend Penny Sanford for her eagle-eyed proofing and editing … Liz Brown, Katie Kruis, Susan Ebbers, Tasia James, and Lindsay Pavel for special support … the BAIPA and NCBPMA Associations for great publishing information … tech wizards Pete Masterson, Rick Calicura, Joanne Berven, and all the folks at Apple for invaluable technical help (it's all magic to me!) … May May Gong of Northwest Digital Designs for a stunning Web site … the dedicated teachers, tutors, and parents who have given so generously of their time, talents, and resources to combat illiteracy … family, friends, and all the original authors from all over the world, whoever they are and wherever they might be (above or under the ground!), for the marvelous collection of proverbs …

Heartfelt and humble thanks to my editor Margie McAneny and the rest of the talented crew at Jossey-Bass/Wiley for sharing my vision and for their enthusiastic support and friendship. I am very grateful.

Last but not least, I want to thank all of **you** for letting this book be part of your lives. It's been **wonderful**!

Love,
Dolores

Introduction

*R*eading is a conversation between a reader and an author. It is our "remote control" to faraway places and long-ago times. The poem on page xi, for example, was written over 700 years ago! If it were not for the written word, every time someone dies an entire library of knowledge would die along with them.

Why Phonics?

Everyone ought to know the joy of decoding an unfamiliar word, syllable by syllable, of exploring the uncharted world of new words and fresh ideas. If we are limited to reading only words we know, and guessing at new words through context clues, we are confined within the boundaries of our current vocabularies and thoughts, interpreting things only from within our own limited perspectives.

When children enter first grade, their comprehension vocabulary is estimated to be upward of 20,000 words. Phonics is the clearest connecting link between this vocabulary and the printed page. After learning these sound-to-symbol skills, most children are able to read almost anything within their speaking and listening vocabularies and interests, unlimited by "readability formulas" or simplified in any other way. It gives students the key to read words they already know, and the skills to look up words they don't know, allowing comprehension to happen. They are able to read the words they could only guess at before, and can focus on the real purpose of reading—*meaning.*

With *direct* or *explicit* phonics the 44 sounds and 200 spelling patterns accounting for the great majority of words in the English language are learned first, one at a time, and gradually combined and recombined into words and sentences. Reading is taught like any other complex skill, such as learning how to dance or play the piano. One note, step, or sound is learned at a time and very gradually combined into more complicated chords, routines, or syllables and words. Sight-reading whole groups of notes at a time, or combining steps into an entire dance routine, or reading whole sentences and books, is what occurs naturally as a *result* of training and practice, and should never be used as a teaching tool in the beginning. Phonics is the process—sight-reading is the result.

Don't Children Have Different Learning Modes?

Children do have different learning modes. Therefore, we have presumed it necessary to tailor reading methods to perceptual styles. No research has ever validated this approach. Studies conclusively prove that letter knowledge and phonemic awareness are the best indicators of reading success. And if a multisensory approach is used to teach phonics, then all students will learn, whether auditory, visual, or kinesthetic. A multisensory method has the synergistic effect of addressing the strongest learning mode while reinforcing the weakest. *How* students learn is different—but *what* students learn should be the same. Every one should be able to decode the longest of unfamiliar words, syllable by syllable, whatever their learning modes.

Don't We Teach Phonics Now?

The most common reading programs today are based on *literature* or *whole language*, whereby students learn to read by being exposed to good classic literature. The premise is that being able to read is a *developmental* skill, as is being able to walk or talk. Words are first learned as wholes—the critical initial step of teaching letter sounds and blending them into syllables is not included. Spelling is not taught in systematic patterns, but taken from the story being read in a random fashion. What if we had to learn mathematics "times tables" randomly, such as 9×7, 12×8, 6×13? It would be most difficult, indeed!

If a student needs assistance with a word, "phonetic hints" are given by naming the beginning and ending letter sounds, but students must then guess to fill in the middle part. Students are also encouraged to guess at words through sentence context clues—story meaning is stressed over word accuracy. It is perfectly acceptable to substitute "house" for "home" because the meaning is the same. But as Mark Twain wrote: "The difference between the right word and the almost right word is the difference between lightning and the lightning bug!"

Consider the words "laparoscopy" and "lobotomy." They each begin and end with the same letters. They each have similar shapes. They each have similar meanings (both are surgical procedures) when taken in general context. Few of us, however, would wish for a surgeon who was only able to read these words by shape, beginning and ending letters, and context clues! With explicit phonics these words are read by syllables: "lap-a-ros-co-py" or "lo-bot-o-my." There is no chance of ever confusing one with the other. There really is a world of difference between being *almost* right and *exactly* right!

Are mistakes like this really made? In Virginia a teacher was recently hired to tutor a licensed pharmacist who could not discern the difference between "chlorpropamide," which lowers blood sugar, and "chlorpromazine," which is an antipsychotic. Similar stories happen all too frequently.

When words are learned individually as wholes, each word is stored in its own "document" in the brain, making retrieval time-consuming and difficult. This frequently results in students' reading slowly and laboriously, and never for pleasure. Progress can remain slow and uncertain. Sometimes the brighter children have more difficulty because their logical minds can rebel unless they are able to connect it all into a framework that makes sense. Trying to teach young children how to read using only a whole-word method can result in highly stressed, fearful youngsters who feel they are failures when they are unable to read.

In summary, **explicit** phonics builds a word from single letters, moving from the *smallest parts to the whole*. **Implicit** phonics teaches the whole word first, moving from the *whole to the smallest parts*. This difference is critical, as they have vastly different results. Some reading programs claim to teach phonics with titles such as "Balanced Reading Program," "Systematic Contextual Phonics," "Embedded Phonics," "Phonemic Awareness," etc. These programs use *implicit phonics,* whereby words are learned as wholes. Since the word "phonics" is so misunderstood, one must always look beyond the title into the reading program itself.

Why is there so much confusion if explicit phonics is so effective? Most likely it is because for more than 40 years we have been without not only phonics texts but also courses in teachers colleges that include this kind of instruction. Most of the classic phonics reading and spelling textbooks have long been out of print.

Almost everyone would agree that "reading for meaning" should be a primary objective with *any* reading method. But how is this goal best achieved? When students are able to effortlessly decode their already considerable comprehension vocabulary, they are joyously freed to "read for meaning" instead of having to struggle while "meaning to read." They can focus on the *meaning* of what they are reading because the *mechanics* of sound-to-symbol relationships have already been learned and practiced until they are automatic.

The brain is not unlike a computer insofar as memory and retrieval are concerned. We might think of explicit phonics as a software program, the logical framework into which patterns and categories of words are organized and filed. Words can be quickly retrieved when reading, and skills do not fade. Learning to read by logical patterns results in clear, precise thinking, a skill that enhances everything children do. Math frequently improves as reading skills are developed, and spelling improves dramatically!

What About Dyslexia?

Dyslexia is a difficult problem, with no easy answers. The original definition described adults who had lost their ability to read following a stroke or injury. Its present usage is more generic, referring to reading disorders known or unknown, frequently resulting in word or letter confusion and/or reversal.

However, it has been my experience in 30 years of tutoring that many students who had been labeled dyslexic no longer reversed letters or words after they were taught explicit phonics. Many were no longer hyperactive. Behavior problems diminished or disappeared.

In medical references, dyslexia is defined as "failure to see or hear similarities or differences in letters or words … tendency to substitute words for those he cannot see …" Guessing! Our students are trained to do the very thing that medical journals define as dyslexic.

A compelling hypothesis is that those students who no longer had dyslexic symptoms after they were taught explicit phonics were not really dyslexic to begin with, but only suffering from a lack in their educational training. Students cannot be expected to know what they may never have been taught, just as teachers cannot teach what they may not know.

Current research shows early letter reversals to be a normal developmental stage for many children. Just as crawling prepares a child for walking, incorporating blending skills when teaching beginning reading will help pattern eyes to move smoothly from left to right across the page, strengthen eye-tracking skills, and prevent or correct reversals. It is *essential* that students receive training in blending letters and syllables when first learning how to read, or to remediate established patterns of reversals!

Many students learn how to read easily and effortlessly after being taught letter sounds and blending skills. Those students who are truly dyslexic need more time and practice to develop fluent reading skills. The time it takes to acquire these skills varies greatly with each child, but the end result is ease and fluency of reading with excellent comprehension—a genuine and effortless enjoyment of all the wonderful stories in today's literature-rich curricula.

What About Invented Spelling?

The idea behind invented spelling is that students will remain free and creative, and "grow into" correct spelling later. But however we learn something the first time tends to "stick," even if it is wrong. For example, if we learn someone's name incorrectly, it seems that we are forever calling that person by that name. It takes some time and effort to correct the error. Recent research has also revealed that accurate spelling is critical to the reading process, and to whatever extent this knowledge is missing, it is strongly associated with specific learning disability. Invented spelling is *not* true freedom!

Is Phonemic Awareness the Same Thing as Phonics?

Phonemic awareness is the ability to hear sounds within a word when it is spoken. It is an *auditory* skill. Recent research has shown it to be the critical first step in learning how to read. Rhyming, singing, and reading aloud to children will help develop this skill. While phonemic awareness is an important *precursor to* phonics, it should never be confused with *instruction in* phonics, which is visual *and* auditory. For example, you could listen to the following word over and over again and thoroughly know the sounds in it. Now try reading it (in Russian!): Рид. How in the world would being phonemically aware of the *sounds* in this word ever be of any help whatsoever in actually *reading* it? Only by knowing the letter-sound relationships can this word ever be correctly read (turn upside down):   Р = r, и = e, д = d. *Read!*

When Should Children Learn How to Read?

Four- to six-year-olds can and should be taught letter sounds and blending skills in order to gain a solid foundation of reading basics. All children this age love to make noises, build things, and take things apart. This is the proper age to teach the letters of the alphabet and the sounds they make, and to begin blending skills!

After that, some children will be able to blend sounds together faster than others. Others may be able to sound out a word rather quickly, but it may be months before they are able to read even short phrases. It may even take some students years to be able to read sentences. It is the ability to put these skills together that allows children to read books, and this varies greatly from child to child. It is a developmental stage that depends upon how mature their nervous systems are, and when their eyes are able to track smoothly from left to right across a page. One thing it has *nothing* to do with is intelligence, any more than wearing glasses does.

Once students have solid phonics skills under their belts, they are ready to begin reading beginning readers. While it's true that schools implementing phonics and literature together do show positive results, it always takes longer to do it that way, with a lot more work on the students' part. The more phonics skills students possess before reading "real" books, the stronger their reading will be. It is my experience that if students wait to read books until they are able to read the *Pyramid* exercise on page 52, they will achieve maximum results in the minimum time with the least amount of effort. Students will then possess the gift of literacy at its most vital and fundamental level—the ability to read with ease, accuracy, fluency, and most of all … *great enjoyment!*

Note: Throughout this book the word "him" refers to male and female students equally.

ABOUT *PHONICS PATHWAYS*

Phonics Pathways is organized by sounds and spelling patterns. They are introduced one at a time and slowly built into words, syllables, phrases, and sentences. Each new step builds upon previously learned skills for continuous review and reinforcement. Learning in small, incremental steps is easier for everyone, especially students with learning disabilities or very short attention spans. A multisensory method is used to address all learning styles.

Short-vowel sounds are presented first—they are the basic foundation that is needed to build good reading and spelling skills. They are best learned in isolation. In the beginning, many children are unable to hear these sounds *within* a word—accordingly, every letter introduced has multiple illustrations of objects *beginning* with its sound. Listening for and identifying these sounds develop phonemic awareness, which is the important first step in learning how to read. Multiple pictures more accurately illustrate the subtle range of sounds that make up each letter—similar in effect to a 3-D hologram.

These sounds and syllables are learned in the same way that we learn math—by pattern, and in order of complexity. Only the simplest and most regular spelling of each sound is presented at first. Spelling variations and sight words are not introduced until basic reading skills are well established. "Red," for example, is learned with other short-vowel, three-letter words on page 41, but "blue" is not introduced until page 169, with other "ue" vowel digraph words, such as "true." This strategy makes learning and assimilation much easier, especially for bilingual students whose primary languages may have only one sound per letter.

Graduated blending exercises are incorporated as part of the teaching technique in this book. These blending exercises ("eyerobics") begin with 17 pages of two-letter blends to establish smooth, strong left-to-right eye-tracking skills. Blending practice is critical to the reading process, and it helps prevent or correct reversals. It also smooths out choppy reading, such as "kuh-a-t" for "cat."

Two-letter blends are integrated into meaningful words as soon as possible, beginning with three-letter words. They are not taught first as a separate set of disconnected skills to memorize before being applied. Memory experts have long known that it is much easier to remember something new if we are able to connect it to something else that is already known. Blending sounds into words we already know also helps prevent the "reading-without-understanding" syndrome sometimes seen when phonograms are learned in isolation. ☆

Two-word phrases build into three-word sentences, etc.—gradually increasing in length and complexity. Many children have difficulty moving directly from words into whole sentences, and they need this gradual transition. Eye span increases as eye tracking strengthens. ☆

Reading and spelling are taught as an integrated unit—teaching them together reinforces and enhances each skill. Accuracy in reading and spelling is taught from the very first lesson.

Phonics Pathways contains all of the spelling rules and is a complete spelling reference. While it is not necessary to know all of these rules in order to read, this knowledge is a real shortcut to spelling accuracy. For example, some words are spelled "-able" and others "-ible," as in "appeasable, visible, taxable, edible"—*why?* Learning one rule for many words is much easier than learning each word individually. An index to these spelling rules is on page 244.

All examples and practice readings are included, which are *100% decodable*—comprising *only* letters, sounds, and rules already learned. This reinforces and cements newly learned skills, as well as developing accuracy and fluency. Using a piano analogy, just because children know the keyboard notes does not mean they are ready to play a lovely sonata! Similarly, just because children know letters and sounds does not mean they are ready to read good literature.

Large, 24-point letters are used for the text. Even with proper glasses students often struggle with smaller letters when learning. Once reading is established, it's easier to read finer print.

The diacritical markings used are consistent with those found in commonly used dictionaries. This knowledge is very handy for dictionary work later on. Using other notation systems would require relearning the dictionary's markings eventually. Why not learn them correctly first?

There is no guessing, and there is no choosing. Guessing is not the same as reading, and even considering a wrong answer takes unnecessary time and energy. What if a music teacher tried to teach you how to play the piano by having you choose the correct note from a list?

Younger children will enjoy Dewey the Bookworm as he guides them through these lessons. Older students and adults will find inspiration in the wise and humorous proverbs sprinkled throughout the book, encouraging virtues such as self-discipline, patience, perseverance, kindness, and personal integrity.

Phonics Pathways is approved for legal compliance with the California Department of Education, enabling school districts to purchase it with Instructional Materials Fund monies. It is an ideal complement to today's literature-based reading programs, providing the tools and teaching skills needed to unlock and decode these wonderful, classic old stories.

William Blake once said:

> *There are things that are known*
> *and things that are unknown …*
> *and in between are only doors.*

Phonics Pathways is the key that will open the door to literacy for *everyone!*

GETTING STARTED

Find a time and place that is quiet and satisfactory for teachers and students. Go slowly, and genuinely praise their efforts. Be gently persistent in working every day—daily practice is essential!

However, do not hurry or pressure your students. There may even be times when it's best to put lessons aside for a while. Many things affect children's receptiveness to learning, such as maturity, attention span, health, hyperactivity, etc. Attention span can vary greatly with each child, and even from day to day with the same child.

Read all of the directions in each lesson before you begin, and *always* do these lessons in sequence. This is important because one skill builds upon another, and each practice reading reflects knowledge of all the letter sounds learned up to that point.

At first, work only a few minutes a day. It is the *habit* of sitting together for a lesson that is important to establish—you will gradually find yourselves spending more time with these lessons. Success breeds confidence and enthusiasm on the students' parts, and a desire to do more. However, lessons never need to be longer than 10 or 15 minutes to show real progress.

Keep studying one lesson until your children know it thoroughly. The goal is not just to impart knowledge, but to make it *automatic* in recall. Reading these letter sounds should not be a conscious effort; it should be as effort-*less* and automatic as saying their own names. Your students should move ahead when they are completely ready—*never* according to "age or page." They might complete several pages in one day, or need many days to complete one page.

Following is a sample lesson plan for teaching the short-vowel sounds. It has proven to be an effective, seven-step strategy for many students, but can be modified or changed in any way.

1. Complete the first lesson on page 10, following the step-by-step directions.

2. Play *Memory*. Find a box with a cover, and let students help you collect things to put into it, such as a pin, ball, eraser, sock, envelope, paper clip, etc. Have them choose one item, feel it, and put it in the box. Close the cover and ask them what is inside. Keep repeating this process, adding one item at a time, until they can no longer name the objects in the same order. This game develops their concentration, memory, and ability to recall images sequentially.

3. Re-read the lesson. Think of words that rhyme with each sound, including nonsense words.

4. Get a book of jokes or riddles, and tell them one—they will enjoy sharing it with friends!

5. Play the *Short-Vowel Shuffle*. (See page 5.) Also, make them a *Short-Vowel Stick* (page 4).

6. Read to them. There are excellent guides available suggesting wonderful books for every age level. Choose books for the beauty of the language, even though they will be beyond their current reading capability—after all, it is good music that inspires us, not piano drills!

7. Reward them. Here are two possibilities to consider:

   (a) Give them each a coin to put in a special jar, but do not let them keep their coins until some agreed-upon time (end of year, birthday, etc.). They may hold and count the coins only at the end of the lesson, while you are reading to them. Remind them that each coin represents a lesson they have had, and that their "bank" of skills is growing along with their "bank" of money.

   (b) Give them each a sticker to put on a 3 × 5 card. Let each student keep the card when it is full and/or trade it in for a prize.

Teaching Tips for Remedial Students:

Use the review pages in the back of each lesson as a pre-test, in order to find out exactly where to begin these lessons. The starting point should be at the place where they are able to work comfortably and accurately, from the very first day. Frequently students do not know the short-vowel sounds or have difficulty blending sounds together. You will determine this when pre-testing.

Tell them everyone needs help with something, and that many famous people had a lot of difficulty learning how to read and write. Explain that it *always* takes more time to unlearn something and re-learn it another way. Understanding these things will help them be a little more patient with themselves.

Use imagery in creative ways. Many of the proverbs in *Phonics Pathways* were chosen especially to be encouraging and meaningful to remedial students—read proverbs to them. Find out the things they enjoy doing, and talk about them. Remedial students need a lot of encouragement!

More Beginning Strategies:

1. Using an overhead projector, have the whole class do the first two steps on page 10 together. Then call on individual students to say the name and beginning sound of the picture you point to—vary the picture, but always include the short sound of "a" as well.

2. Next, write a large "Aa" on the chalkboard. Trace each letter three times, naming its short sound out loud with the class each time. Repeat this exercise, this time having the students trace large letters on their desktops with their fingertips as you trace these letters on the board. Complete the remaining steps on page 10, and repeat with the rest of the vowels.

3. Write all vowels in large letters in a horizontal line on the chalkboard and draw vertical lines between them. Dictate a vowel sound to your students and have them write it under the correct column, name it, and repeat the short sound of that vowel. (See also number 2 on page 255.)

ant   exercise   itch   octopus   umbrella

4. Make copies of the master "Short Sheet of Vowels" on page 256, and give a copy to each student. Dictate a sound, and ask students to write the letter in the correct column. Continue doing this exercise with blends and short-vowel words—it's great reinforcement.

5. Make a master sheet of the *Short-Vowel Stick* shown on the previous page. Run off enough copies for every student, laminate, and cut them out. Each student should keep a *Short-Vowel Stick* on the desk at all times during reading lessons as a quick reference. It is an indispensable teaching tool!

6. Students enjoy using this *Short-Vowel Stick* as a bookmark as well, and also find it very handy to put underneath the word or sentence they are reading to help guide them across the page.

7. Be sure to check out all the tips, charts, activities, and games beginning on page 255! These reproducibles are invaluable strategies that will greatly enhance your teaching in many different ways. The record-keeping sheets will prove extremely useful as well.

The **SHORT-VOWEL SHUFFLE** (shown on the next page) is played one-on-one with the teacher, in small groups, or with a whole class. This card game reviews and reinforces the short-vowel sounds, and is especially appropriate for younger students. Older students and adults will find these cards quite useful as flash cards to reinforce learning and speed up the recognition-response time. Either way, they are *very* helpful!

Copy the next page, and run off four or more copies on colored cardstock. Laminate and cut them apart. Begin with the "**a**" cards, and add more short-vowel cards as they are learned. Use all of the "eyes" cards. Shuffle the cards and place them facedown on the middle of the table. Use several or many sets of cards, depending upon the number of vowels being played and how much time there is for playing.

1. Take turns drawing a card from the top of the stack. Students trace it with their fingertips (on the card or on their desktops), read the sound out loud, and lay each card face up on the table.

2. Whenever an "eyes" card is turned over, one of the following things happens:

   (a) students "shuffle" once around their desks and sit down again (show them how to shuffle!),

   (b) the teacher holds his or her nose and says, "**HONK**,"

   (c) students jump up and down like a jack-in-the-box, or

   (d) whatever else was agreed upon beforehand—use your own imagination!

3. Continue playing the game until all of the cards have been drawn and read.

Miscellaneous:

Exactly *how much* of this book must students learn in order to read, and *how long* will it take? Some students begin reading on their own very early in the book, while others need to learn many more rules and spelling patterns (*especially* students with learning disabilities) before being able to read with ease. It varies greatly.

i

e

u

a

o

This can be dramatically illustrated by looking at the results of a two-year pilot study using *Phonics Pathways* as an in-school tutoring program. Forty to 60 remedial students ranging from first to fourth grade participated. Parent volunteers tutored each student about three times a week, in 20-minute sessions. These students required from 7 to 184 tutoring sessions in order to read at or near grade level. The following chart summarizes this activity:

GRADE LEVEL OF STUDENTS	SKILL LEVEL MASTERED RESULTING IN READING AT OR CLOSE TO GRADE LEVEL	PAGE	AVERAGE NO. OF TUTORING SESSIONS
1st Grade	Two-Consonant Endings Review	69	50
2nd Grade	Long-Vowel Review	105	77
3rd & 4th Grade	Two-Consonant Beginnings Review	147	94

However, long after your students are reading, they should continue using this book for ongoing development and fluency in reading and spelling. Knowing these spelling rules, shortcuts, tips, and diacritical marks for dictionary work will give them a real "educational edge"!

While most students enjoy the humorous and encouraging proverbs, some of these sayings may be too sophisticated for the youngest to appreciate. You will be able to determine this as you work through the book.

Are any of your children clumsy, tired a lot, impulsive, and/or hyperactive? Do they have short attention spans and/or poor coordination? These children frequently have learning problems. Among the many causes of these symptoms *may* be allergies and sensitivities, which some specialists feel can take a systemic form instead of a more common, localized form, such as hay fever. Experts disagree whether this can be a factor. But you might consider asking your doctor for a safe elimination diet for these students to try, and see if it makes a difference. At the very *least* you can try to avoid junk foods, or those with a lot of chemical additives. It makes a real difference with many children, and just might be worth trying!

Could your students have vision problems, even though they may not need glasses? Some experts feel that if children are clumsy and have poor coordination and/or reverse letters, they could also benefit from exercises designed to help eyes move together from left to right, and to improve motor coordination skills. The premise is that developing these skills is very helpful to the reading process. Experts disagree, but in my experience it has been beneficial to many students. Pages 251 and 252 contain some excellent and effective vision and motor coordination training exercises that are frequently prescribed by specialists when treating dyslexia. And, of course, left-to-right eye tracking is part of the teaching technique used throughout this book.

There will be many more teaching tips as you work through the book. Good luck, have fun, and remember—these times together should be an *enjoyable* learning experience for *all of you!*

ABOUT DEWEY

Dewey first made his appearance many years ago, in a secret note passed to my best friend Mary Lou in a third-grade classroom. At that time he was called "The Burp," and he underwent many exciting adventures during the next few years before being retired for more worldly pursuits, such as roller skating, fishing with Dad, reading fairy tales and Greek myths with Mom, and dressing up and parading around in my aunt's beautiful, sparkling, colorful old Ziegfeld Follies costumes found hidden in an old steamer trunk in a dusty corner of the attic.

The Burp was resurrected a few years ago when I was requested to design and create a large bookworm, to be submitted to the citywide Harvest Festival doll competition representing the Livermore Public Library. He was carefully redesigned, receiving form and substance as a six-foot-tall, pink and green fuzzy striped bookwork. Dewey D. System, *Bookwormus Giganticus,* was thrilled (and yes, a bit pompous!) when he won first prize.

For a brief but glorious time, Dewey reigned supreme on a bookcase in the Friend's Corner of the Livermore library, holding court with large throngs of admiring fans. He loved everyone, but *especially* the children. He tended to dissect and categorize when feeling playful, but pun terribly when feeling peevish. He fed late at night, long after the library had closed. He devoured books primarily, but was able to digest almost any variety of food for thought. Mostly he loved chewing on tasty, meaty things such as great big fat cookbooks, but confessed to nibbling spicy tidbits

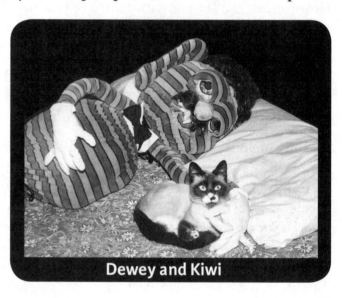

Dewey and Kiwi

on the odd occasion. However, Dewey choked on political items of *any* flavor. For dessert he relished consuming dense, nutty but half-baked trifles, filled with dates.

Unfortunately, Dewey then began crunching Apples. He gobbled bits and bytes out of the mouse, RAM, and any tasty cookie chips he found on the menu. Sad to say, he also sipped the port. He finally crashed with a system virus, and was politely requested to leave the library.

Dewey came back home to live, having earned a much-deserved and honorable retirement. He adores munching snacks and taking long naps with Kiwi, regaling her with tall tales about his glory days as a blue-ribbon-prize winner. But sometimes—every once in a while—he gets a faraway look in his eyes, and seems a little sad and wistful. I wonder if, at those times, he might be dimly recalling those long-ago days when he was just a little Burp, sharing so many rousing adventures with two small, shy third-grade girls. I wonder …

… what do **YOU** think?

—Dolores

And now ...

Whatever you CAN do or DREAM

you can ...

BEGIN IT!

—Goethe

SHORT-VOWEL SOUNDS

We shall begin by learning the *short sounds* of the five vowels in the English language. We shall learn them one at a time, beginning with the letter "a." Try to spend just a few minutes, once or twice a day, learning these sounds.

1. *Listen carefully* while your teacher reads the name and beginning sound of each picture on the next page, including the letter **a**. *Especially* notice the beginning sound. (The *name* of the letter is **a**, and the *sound* of the letter is shown as /ă/.) Try closing your eyes for better concentration:

> "Atom /ă/, apple /ă/, ant /ă/, A /ă/.
> /Ă/ is the short sound of the letter A."

2. If you closed your eyes, now open them while your teacher reads these pictures and sounds again. This time *you* say these pictures and sounds along *with* her:

> "Atom /ă/, apple /ă/, ant /ă/, A /ă/."

3. Read the name and short sound of "a" and trace each letter with your fingertip. Make sure you start at the correct place and move in the correct direction. Various writing pads or workbooks can show you how to do this.

4. Now *write* the letter and say this sound again. (If writing is too difficult, trace a big letter on the tabletop or in the air with your fingertip, or just point. See page 252 for exercises that will help develop writing dexterity.)

5. Read the review in the window box at the bottom, then write it from dictation.

6. Play the *Short-Vowel Shuffle* on page 5. It helps you learn and is fun to play!

7. Repeat these instructions with each of the four remaining vowels.

And now—let us meet **Dewey**, a truly wise bookworm who will be your personal guide throughout this book. He adds his own inspiration and special thoughts to encourage you along the way.

Have you ever met a lot of people at the same time? It was very DIFFICULT to remember all of their names, wasn't it? Perhaps you couldn't. But when you meet people just ONE AT A TIME, it is so much easier.

It is the same thing when learning how to read, or when learning to do almost ANYTHING, for that matter. Just learn one small thing at a time, then another, and just keep on going. And before you know it, YOU will know it!

Aă Aă

There are TWO WAYS of writing "a."

Here is how we READ it: "a"

And here is how we WRITE it: "a"

"Atom /ă/, apple /ă/, ant /ă/, A /ă/."

The little mark you see above each of these letters is called a DIACRITICAL mark. This is the diacritical mark for a short-vowel sound. There are different marks for different sounds.

These marks tell you exactly how to pronounce letters and syllables. They are the *key* that shows you how to sound out a word when you look it up in the dictionary.

Knowing this code is *very handy!*

a   a

Eĕ

H E L L oooooooooooooooooooooooooooooooooo

... *Hello!*

If it's TOO HARD for you to hear these sounds clearly from dictation, try saying the sound out loud yourself, after hearing it. It may be helpful. Do this for as long as you need to.

Play the Short-Vowel Shuffle (page 5) with the "a" and "e" cards, and keep adding more letter cards as you learn them. It's a lot of FUN!

"Echo /ĕ/, exercise /ĕ/, evergreen /ĕ/, edge /ĕ/, E /ĕ/."

Educators such as Maria Montessori have long known that when we use *all* of our senses to learn something, it's easier to learn and remember. That is why we *see, hear, say, feel,* and *write* each letter that we are learning. This is called a MULTISENSORY method of learning, and it makes things so much easier. It's really amazing, when you stop to think about it!

a   e   a

Iĭ

It can be really difficult to tell these sounds apart at first.

Here's a neat trick that many people find very helpful (as well as fun to do!):

Let's suppose that you are having trouble telling **i** from **e**.

Try saying the **e** pictures using the **i** sound: "icho, ixercise, ivergreen, idge."

Now say the **i** pictures with the **e** sound: "etch, egloo." See what I mean?

This little ~~ixercise~~ exercise is helpful because when you listen to both the WRONG and RIGHT way of saying these sounds in a word, it's EASIER to hear the difference!

"Itch /ĭ/, igloo /ĭ/, I /ĭ/."

The *highest mountain*
in the whole world
is still climbed
by taking only
one small step at a time, and keeping on going …

Just as we are learning how to read by taking only one small step at a time, and keeping on going!

a   e   i   a

O ŏ

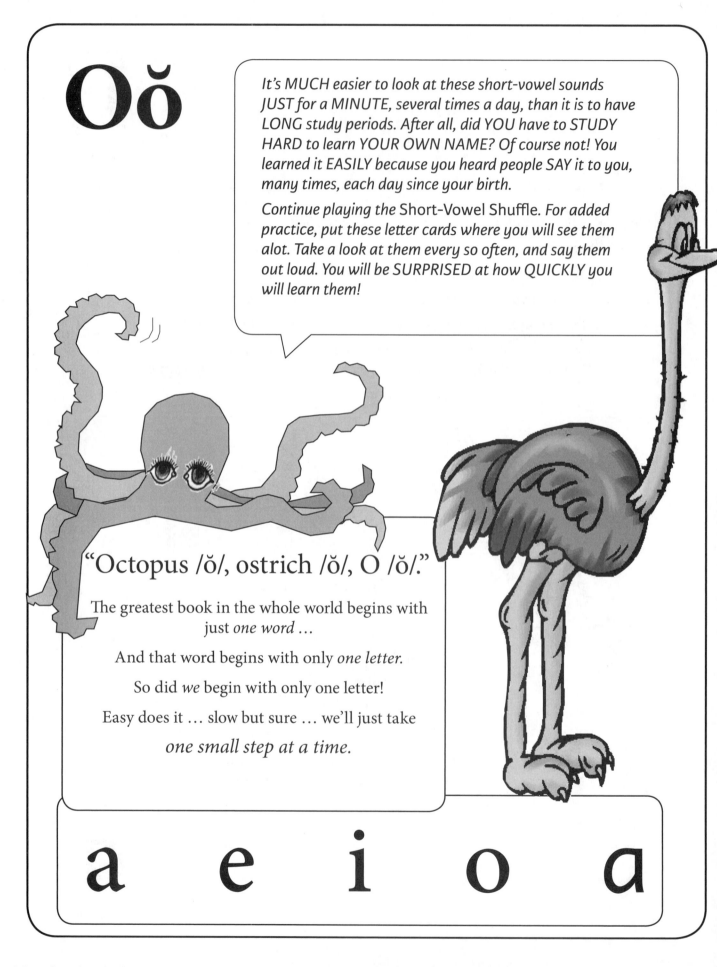

It's MUCH easier to look at these short-vowel sounds JUST for a MINUTE, several times a day, than it is to have LONG study periods. After all, did YOU have to STUDY HARD to learn YOUR OWN NAME? Of course not! You learned it EASILY because you heard people SAY it to you, many times, each day since your birth.

Continue playing the Short-Vowel Shuffle. For added practice, put these letter cards where you will see them alot. Take a look at them every so often, and say them out loud. You will be SURPRISED at how QUICKLY you will learn them!

"Octopus /ŏ/, ostrich /ŏ/, O /ŏ/."

The greatest book in the whole world begins with just *one word* ...

And that word begins with only *one letter*.

So did *we* begin with only one letter!

Easy does it ... slow but sure ... we'll just take

one small step at a time.

a e i o a

Uŭ

"Ugly /ŭ/, up /ŭ/, umbrella /ŭ/, U /ŭ/."

And that ends the vowels! On the next page is your first review. Remember one thing when reviewing: *don't ever guess!* A wrong answer leaves an imprint on your brain, which then takes *more* time and energy to *unlearn*.

Always look back at the letter pictures until you know these sounds well enough not to. It makes things easier—and in the long run, you will learn *faster!*

a   e   i   o   u

Short-Vowel Review (Bingo)

Read the letters and short sounds of these vowels once a day. Then write them from dictation under the correct vowel heading on the "Short Sheet of Vowels" (page 256). Also play number one (Echo) and two (All in a Row) on the Hot Tips page (250) to help develop phonemic awareness, or play *Bingo*:

SHORT-VOWEL BINGO: Make three copies of this page. Use one copy as a board, and cut the other two copies into letter squares. Place the squares in a pile upside down in the middle of the table. Pick a card, read the sound out loud, and place it over the correct letter on the board. The first one to fill in all the letters in a row wins. Or, play until *both* players win—it's much less pressure. (Also—*heh heh*—it's added practice. *Sneaky!*)

Look back at the letter pictures as often as necessary, but do not proceed until you know these sounds as well as you know your own name.

TEACHING TIPS: Pantomime a word for any sound your learners may have forgotten: bite an apple (/ă/), lift an arm up and down (/ě/ exercise), scratch yourself (/ĭ/ itch), wave your arms around (/ŏ/ octopus), or point upward (/ŭ/ up).

a	i	e	a	o
u	a	o	e	i
i	u	a	a	e
o	e	a	i	u
e	a	o	e	i

Two-Letter Blends (Eyerobics)

Now we shall learn some CONSONANTS and combine them with vowels to make two-letter blends. A consonant is any letter that is not a vowel.

Being able to blend letters together smoothly is a *very important skill!* It will train your eye muscles to track (move) together effortlessly from left to right across the page, so that you will be able to read words and books easily, without having to struggle. Blending practice is good exercise—it is aerobics for the eyes. In fact, let's call it *eye-robics* because that's what it is—aerobics for the eyes!

Eyerobics begins with 17 pages of two-letter blends, gradually building up to long words made of many syllables. A syllable is the smallest part a word can be broken into that also contains a vowel—usually two- or three-letter blends. We build bricks to make *houses,* and syllables to make *words.*

Blending exercises must be practiced in order to become automatic, just like any other skill, such as riding a bicycle. For some students this will take longer than with others.

1. If blending is difficult:

   Practice the blending game on page 20. This *Train Game* is extremely helpful to anyone needing help in learning this skill! There is also a master *Train Game* in the appendix on pages 258 and 259 that is blank, for those of you who wish to continue this exercise with other letters as well.

2. If blending is easy:

   Skip the *Train Game* and continue the blending exercises until the end of this section of *Phonics Pathways.*

3. If blending is especially easy and effortless:

   If blending is super-easy for you, *and* if you already know all the consonant sounds, you may skip the rest of the two-letter blending exercises and move on to the review on page 37. You can either read the blends as they are, or play *StarSearch* to review them for variety. It's good practice, and fun to play!

Did you know that sometimes very intelligent people can have real difficulty when learning how to blend letters together smoothly when reading?

Blending skills have nothing to do with intelligence, any more than wearing glasses does!

Directions

1. Name each picture on the page, and listen for its beginning sound. Each picture begins with the sound of the consonant introduced on that page. (The names of these pictures also contain many sounds you have not had yet, but you are to listen *only* for the *beginning sound* of each one.)

2. Now *blend* the consonant sound with the vowel sound. Begin at the top of the ladder, and read the short "a." Then read the two sounds individually as you move across the page: "s—a." Now blend the two sounds together. Take a *DEEP BREATH* and *STRETCH* the sounds out as you read them, smoothly blending the sound of one letter into the other:

"ssssssaaaaaaaaaaaa"

3. Link this blend with a real word, such as "sa" as in "sat, Sam, sad," etc. Continue in this manner with the rest of the vowels, moving down the page.

4. Read the blends in the review window at the bottom. Keep your *Short-Vowel Stick* handy (page 4) as a quick reference to short-vowel sounds.

5. Write these blends from dictation on **THE SHORT SHEET OF VOWELS** (page 256), under the correct vowel heading. You will soon see which vowels need extra help. (Tip: say the blends to yourself first.) It's *great* reinforcement!

6. Repeat these instructions with the rest of the consonants in this section.

7. If blending is too much of a challenge for you in the beginning, practice the *Train Game* on page 20. It's a hands-on activity that's sure to help!

Spend about 10 minutes a day with this section. You might complete several pages in one day, or you might spend several days on one page. It is how much *time* you spend that counts, not how many *pages* you do!

We review each step a LOT because we need to know this material at a deep level until it's automatic in recall, just as we know our own names. It's like learning how to ride a bicycle, or drive a car: at first, we need to go VERY SLOWLY and think about every step involved. We would NEVER think of going out on a busy freeway or down a steep hill our first time out. That comes later, when our skills are practiced enough to be automatic. THEN it's FUN!

Ss

a	s-a	sa
e	s-e	se
i	s-i	si
o	s-o	so
u	s-u	su

These exercises are excellent practice! But if this page is too DIFFICULT for you, play the Train Game on the next page first. Keep playing it until blending becomes easier for you. (However, if these pages seem too EASY for you, and if you already know the consonant sounds, you may proceed directly to the review on page 37.)

su   so   si   se   sa

se   su   sa   so   si

The *Train Game* game provides intensive kinesthetic eye-tracking practice, helping to prevent or correct reversals. Copy and laminate this page, and cut the letters apart.

1. Place the "s" and "a" cars on the table, with the "s" car on your left and the "a" car on your right, about one or two feet apart.

2. "Chug" the "s" car slightly toward the center with your left hand. Look at it while you slide it, and say its sound at the same time.

3. Now focus your attention on the "a" car. Look at it and chug it slightly toward the center, saying its short sound while you are watching it.

4. Keep going in this fashion, until the cars meet. When the cars "hitch" together, the sounds should hitch together also, in one smooth blend. Be sure that you always *look* at each letter or blend while you *say* it.

(There is a master *Train Game* on pages 258–259 to use with other letters if desired.)

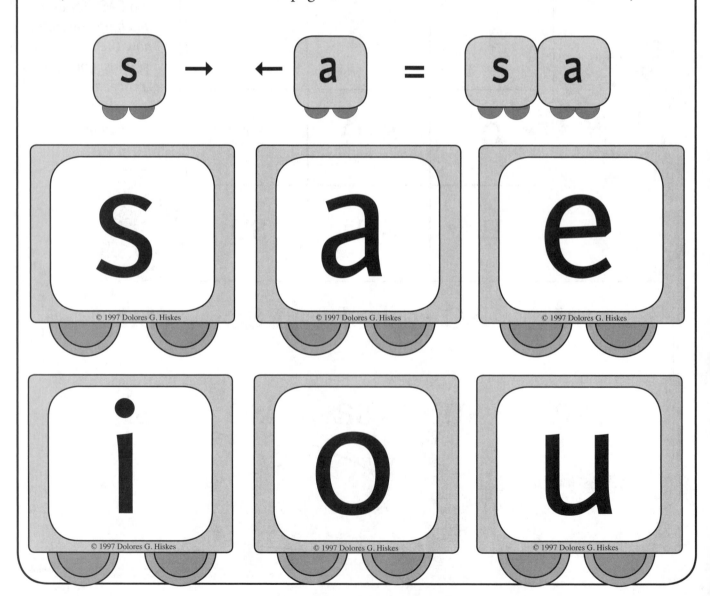

Phonics Pathways: Clear Steps to Easy Reading and Perfect Spelling

Mm

a	m-a	ma
e	m-e	me
i	m-i	mi
o	m-o	mo
u	m-u	mu

SHOOT for the MOON! EVEN if you MISS, you'll eventually land among the STARS!

mu   mo   mi   me   ma

se   sa   su   si

Moon, mouse, mittens

Nn

a	n-a	na
e	n-e	ne
i	n-i	ni
o	n-o	no
u	n-u	nu

When in DOUBT, do the FRIENDLIEST thing!

nu   no   ni   ne   na

su   mi   sa   se

Notes, net, nurse

Rr

a	r-a	ra
e	r-e	re
i	r-i	ri
o	r-o	ro
u	r-u	ru

EVERYONE
has
a
RAINY
CORNER
in
his
life!

ru   ro   ri   re   ra

na   se   mu   ni

ra   ra-n   ran

Rain, ring, rabbit

Ll

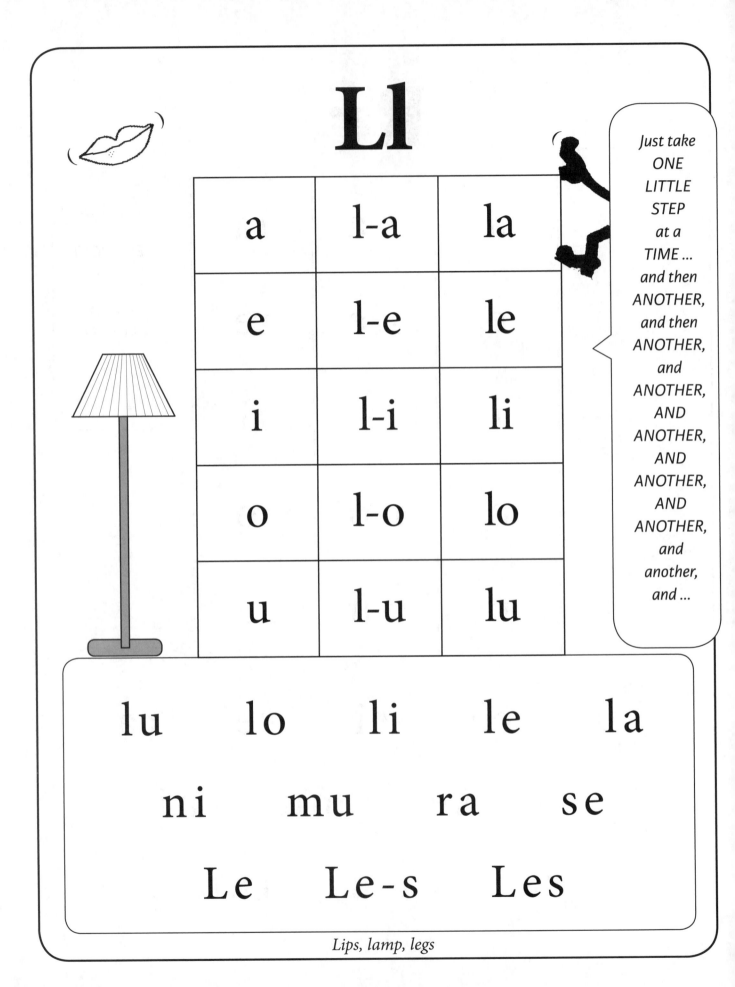

a	l-a	la
e	l-e	le
i	l-i	li
o	l-o	lo
u	l-u	lu

Just take ONE LITTLE STEP at a TIME ... and then ANOTHER, and then ANOTHER, and ANOTHER, AND ANOTHER, AND ANOTHER, AND ANOTHER, and another, and ...

lu   lo   li   le   la

ni   mu   ra   se

Le   Le-s   Les

Lips, lamp, legs

Ff

a	f-a	fa
e	f-e	fe
i	f-i	fi
o	f-o	fo
u	f-u	fu

Remember— when reading these blends also think of some words that BEGIN with these sounds:

/fu/ as in "fun,"
/fo/ as in "fox,"
/fi/ as in "fish," etc.

(How many different words can YOU think of?)

fu   fo   fi   fe   fa

ru   se   lo   ni

fu   fu-n   fun

Flower, finger, fish

Hh

a	h-a	ha
e	h-e	he
i	h-i	hi
o	h-o	ho
u	h-u	hu

We ALL have UNEXPLORED TERRITORY ... it's under our HATS!

hu   ho   hi   he   ha

ra   fe   si   mu

hi   hi-m   him

Heart, handshake, hat

Dd

a	d-a	da
e	d-e	de
i	d-i	di
o	d-o	do
u	d-u	du

It's NICE to be IMPORTANT ... But it's MORE IMPORTANT to be NICE!

du   do   di   de   da

ne   mi   ho   su

Da   Da-n   Dan

Dolphin, drops, dog

Bb

It's MUCH BETTER
to spend just a
FEW MINUTES
A DAY
with this book, rather
than studying
LONGER,
but only
SEVERAL TIMES
A WEEK.
It's like brushing
your teeth ...
They wouldn't look
NEARLY
as nice if you
brushed them only
TWICE A WEEK
but for LONGER,
would they?

a	b-a	ba
e	b-e	be
i	b-i	bi
o	b-o	bo
u	b-u	bu

bu	bo	bi	be	ba
du	ne	mi	fa	
bu	bu-n	bun		

Bees, bear, butterfly

Pp

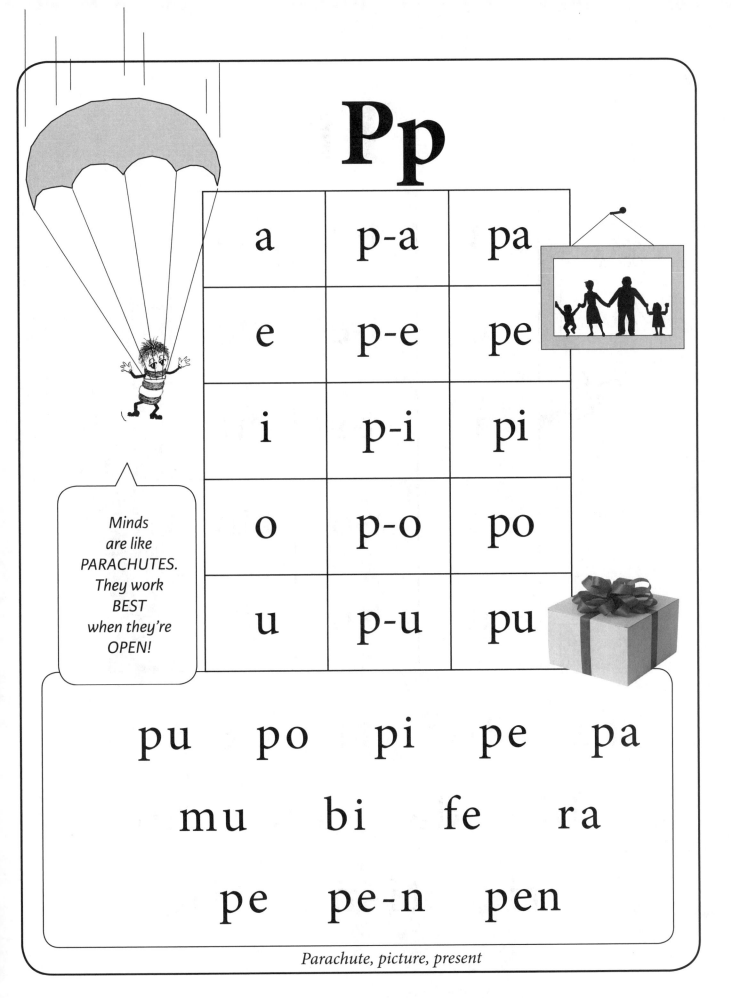

a	p-a	pa
e	p-e	pe
i	p-i	pi
o	p-o	po
u	p-u	pu

Minds are like PARACHUTES. They work BEST when they're OPEN!

pu po pi pe pa

mu bi fe ra

pe pe-n pen

Parachute, picture, present

Tt

The BEST ANGLE from which to approach ANY PROBLEM is the "TRY-ANGLE"!

a	t-a	ta
e	t-e	te
i	t-i	ti
o	t-o	to
u	t-u	tu

tu   to   ti   te   ta

bi   da   nu   ho

ti   ti-n   tin

Triangle, tree, tape

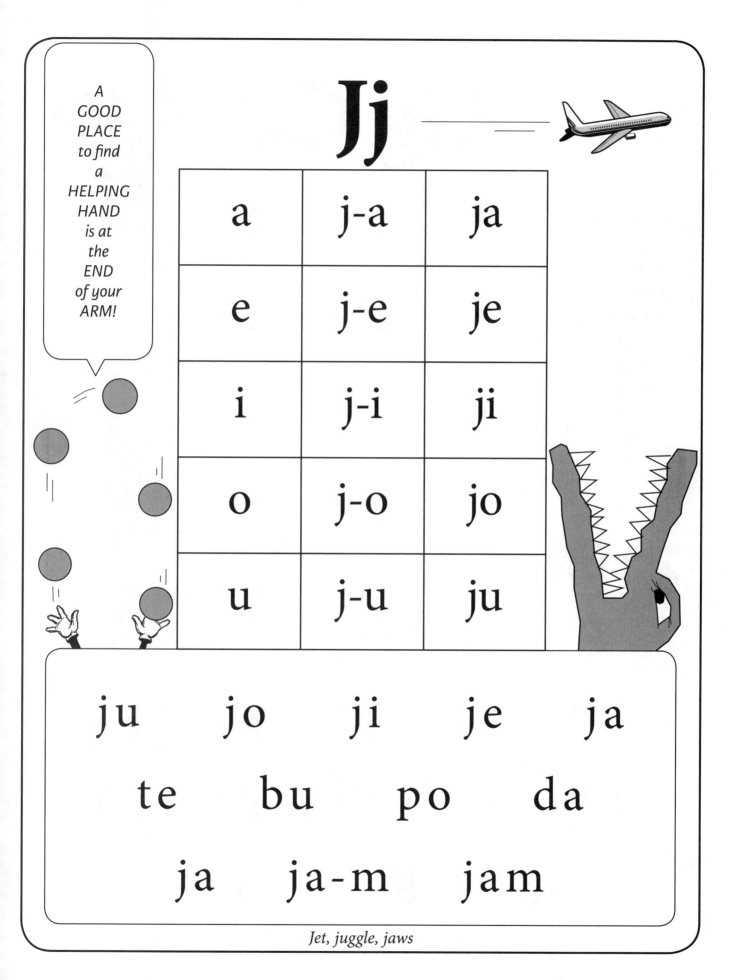

Jj

a	j-a	ja
e	j-e	je
i	j-i	ji
o	j-o	jo
u	j-u	ju

ju   jo   ji   je   ja

te   bu   po   da

ja   ja-m   jam

Jet, juggle, jaws

Gg Gg

a	g-a	ga
e	g-e	ge
i	g-i	gi
o	g-o	go
u	g-u	gu

We READ the letter "g" THIS way: "g" and we WRITE it THIS way: "g"

gu	go	gi	ge	ga
gu	go	gi	ge	ga

ga	ga-s	gas

Grapes, glasses, goblet

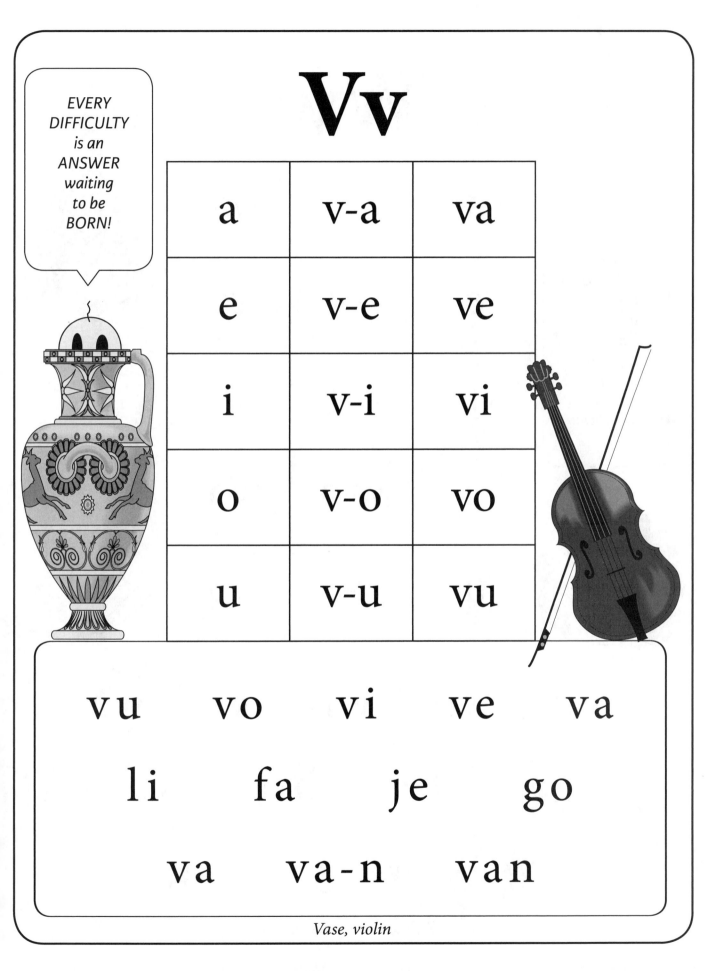

Vv

EVERY DIFFICULTY is an ANSWER waiting to be BORN!

a	v-a	va
e	v-e	ve
i	v-i	vi
o	v-o	vo
u	v-u	vu

vu   vo   vi   ve   va

li   fa   je   go

va   va-n   van

Vase, violin

Ww

a	w-a	wa
e	w-e	we
i	w-i	wi
o	w-o	wo
u	w-u	wu

You will never get AHEAD of anyone as long as you are trying to get EVEN with them!

wu   wo   wi   we   wa

ga   te   bo   su

wa   wa-g   wag

Waffles, wink, watermelon

Yy

The BEST THING to do BEHIND a person's BACK is to PAT IT!

a	y-a	ya
e	y-e	ye
i	y-i	yi
o	y-o	yo
u	y-u	yu

yu yo yi ye ya

wi pa gu de

ya ya-p yap

Yo-yo, yell

Phonics Pathways: Clear Steps to Easy Reading and Perfect Spelling **35**

Zz

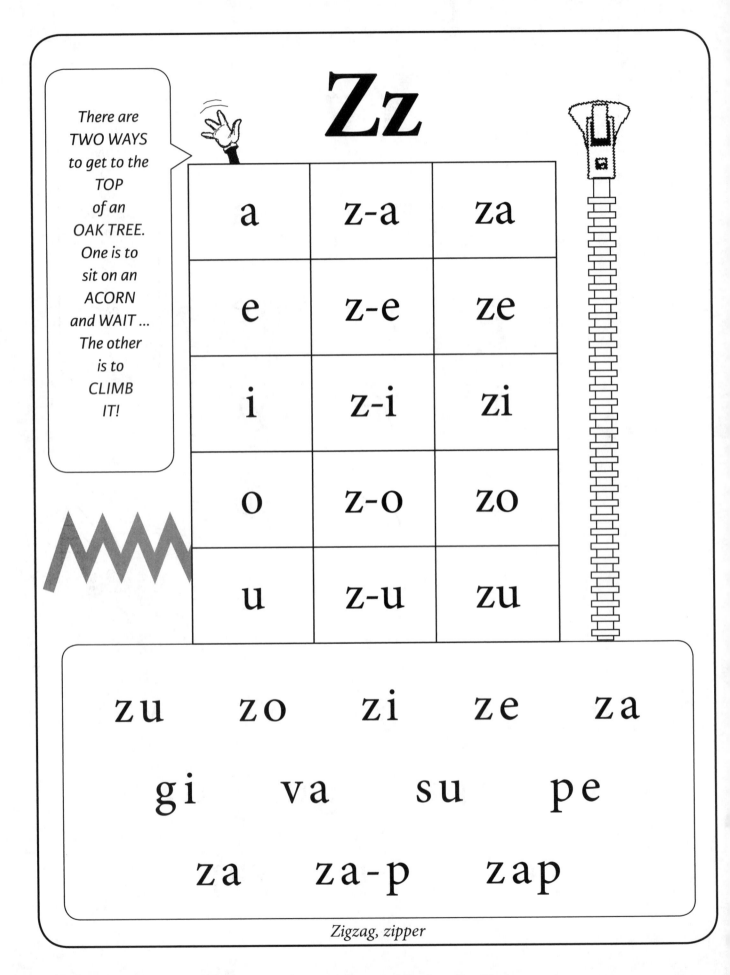

There are TWO WAYS to get to the TOP of an OAK TREE. One is to sit on an ACORN and WAIT ... The other is to CLIMB IT!

a	z-a	za
e	z-e	ze
i	z-i	zi
o	z-o	zo
u	z-u	zu

zu   zo   zi   ze   za

gi   va   su   pe

za   za-p   zap

Zigzag, zipper

Two-Letter Blend Review

You may review these blends either by reading them directly or by playing *StarSearch* astarting on this page. (A *StarSearch* master copy is on page 261.)

Read and write these blends once a day until you can do so easily. Use the "Short Sheet of Vowels" exercise on page 256 for dictation (see page 5 for directions), or copy them after reading them if writing is too much of a challenge just yet.)

And remember: it isn't enough just to sound out each letter individually, as in "s—a", you must blend them both together into one smooth sound:

"sssssaaaaaaaaaaaa"

Look back at the letter pictures as often as you need to, so that you are *thinking it through*, and *not guessing!*

StarSearch

1. Make several copies of the *StarSearch* game pieces on the next page, on cardstock. Copy, laminate, and cut apart all of the cards.

2. Place as many letters and stars cards as you wish to play with on the middle of the table in a pile, upside down. Shuffle to mix them up.

3. Take turns drawing a card and reading it out loud, blending the letters together in one smooth blend.

4. Return all letter cards to the table, but keep the stars cards you pick up. The player with the most stars cards wins!

TEACHING TIPS:

1. *When writing these lessons, try using a whiteboard with a dry-erase marking pen. It's easy to wipe clean and try again when first learning!*

2. *Having trouble telling "b" from "d"? Make a copy of this "bed" card, and keep it handy as a quick reference. The "b" MUST face to the RIGHT, and the "d" MUST face to the LEFT in order to hold the mattress up!*

se	fa	ro	hu
mi	ta	di	bo
na	pe	gi	ju
yu	ba	de	zi
le	vo	wu	po

Three-Letter Words

Eyerobics continues by adding consonants to the ends of two-letter blends to build three-letter words, and then combining two words to make a phrase.

Read each sound and blend, working across the page. When these blends are written with a hyphen between them like this, "s-a," read each sound separately. When they are written without a line between them, as in "sa," you must *blend* the sounds together *smoothly*. It can help to take a deep breath first.

Take all the time you need in order to read each three-letter word *without* having to sound out individual letters first. The time this takes will vary; it depends upon how soon your eye muscles are strong enough to "track" across a word. It does *not* depend upon how *smart* you are!

Now listen to these words and write them from dictation, using the "Short Sheet of Vowels" exercise on page 256. Make sure to write the words under the correct columns! If dictation is still difficult, then copy them from the page—just the actual word will do, not the two-letter blend.

Work about ten minutes a day with these lessons. Take all the time you need in order to read these words *without* having to sound out each letter first.

TEACHING TIPS: Do your eyes sometimes "skip" and "jump around" when reading? Put the *Short-Vowel Stick* or a sheet of paper underneath the *line* you are reading and move your finger underneath each *word* as you read it.

Still having trouble? Try this: cut out a rectangle in a plain sheet of paper, about 3/8 inches high by 6 inches wide. Lay it over the page, so that only the line you are trying to read is showing through the little "window." These little tricks can make reading a *lot* easier! Use them as long as you find it helpful.

Can't wait to read "real books"? Please finish these lessons at least through page 51 *before* trying to read books! Even the best of phonics readers have some sight words in them, and while some students have no trouble with this, many others do. Remedial readers especially need to have phonics skills firmly established prior to combining phonetically decodable words with sight words. It's safe to say that most students should be able to read the *Pyramid* exercise on page 52 before moving on to real readers. Then students may begin with simple, highly decodable readers.

Do you know the definition of PATIENCE?

PATIENCE is being able to IDLE YOUR MOTOR when you REALLY feel like STRIPPING YOUR GEARS!

Reading across the page, slowly blend these letters into three-letter words. Then read the two-word phrases. (A phrase is just a part of a sentence.)

Now copy or write a few words from dictation, if you can—or you might even try writing a phrase! (If you find this page helpful, there are more exercises like this on page 253.)

If you still find blending a challenge, continue playing the Train Game on pages 258 and 259. It will help a lot, and make it much easier to acquire this skill!

a	s-a	sa	sa-t	sat
e	s-e	se	se-t	set
i	s-i	si	si-p	sip
o	s-o	so	so-b	sob
u	s-u	su	su-n	sun

sis sat   sun set

a	a	j-a	ja	ja-m	jam
e	e	j-e	je	je-t	jet
i	i	J-i	Ji	Ji-m	Jim
o	o	j-o	jo	jo-g	jog
u	u	j-u	ju	ju-g	jug

Jim jog   jam jug

Ss

sa	sa-d	sad
se	se-t	set
si	si-t	sit
so	so-b	sob
su	su-n	sun

Ff

fa	fa-d	fad
fe	fe-d	fed
fi	fi-n	fin
fo	fo-p	fop
fu	fu-n	fun

Rr

ra	ra-p	rap
re	re-d	red
ri	ri-b	rib
ro	ro-t	rot
ru	ru-g	rug

Hh

ha	ha-t	hat
he	he-n	hen
hi	hi-d	hid
ho	ho-t	hot
hu	hu-g	hug

sun fun   red hat

Mm

ma	ma-n	man
me	me-t	met
mi	mi-d	mid
mo	mo-p	mop
mu	mu-g	mug

Nn

na	na-g	nag
ne	ne-t	net
ni	ni-p	nip
no	no-d	nod
nu	nu-t	nut

Dd

da	da-d	dad
de	de-n	den
di	di-g	dig
do	do-t	dot
du	du-d	dud

Bb

ba	ba-d	bad
be	be-t	bet
bi	bi-g	big
bo	bo-p	bop
bu	bu-n	bun

You can't be a SMART COOKIE with a CRUMMY ATTITUDE!

big mug   dig nut

Be CAREFUL when you **STRETCH** the TRUTH ...
sometimes it can SNAP BACK like a RUBBER BAND!

Tt

ta	ta-p	tap
te	te-n	ten
ti	ti-n	tin
to	to-p	top
tu	tu-g	tug

Pp

pa	pa-n	pan
pe	pe-n	pen
pi	pi-n	pin
po	po-t	pot
pu	pu-n	pun

Gg

ga	ga-p	gap
ge	ge-t	get
gi	gi-g	gig
go	go-t	got
gu	gu-m	gum

Jj

ja	ja-m	jam
je	je-t	jet
Ji	Ji-m	Jim
jo	jo-g	jog
ju	ju-g	jug

jam pot   top jet

Ll

la	la-p	lap
le	le-g	leg
li	li-p	lip
lo	lo-t	lot
lu	lu-g	lug

Vv

va	va-n	van
va	va-t	vat
ve	ve-t	vet
vi	vi-m	vim

Our lives would run a lot more smoothly if SECOND THOUGHTS came FIRST!

Ww

wa	wa-g	wag
we	we-t	wet
we	we-b	web
wi	wi-n	win
wi	wi-g	wig

Yy

ya	ya-m	yam
ya	ya-p	yap
ye	ye-t	yet
yi	yi-p	yip
yu	yu-m	yum

win van   lug yam

Aa

da	da-d	dad
na	na-g	nag
sa	sa-p	sap
ra	ra-n	ran
ma	ma-d	mad

Ee

pe	pe-p	pep
be	be-g	beg
te	te-n	ten
ge	ge-t	get
ne	ne-t	net

Ii

si	si-s	sis
di	di-p	dip
bi	bi-t	bit
wi	wi-n	win
fi	fi-g	fig

JUMPING TO CONCLUSIONS is not HALF as good an exercise as DIGGING FOR FACTS!

Oo

to	to-t	tot
mo	mo-p	mop
ro	ro-t	rot
ho	ho-t	hot
do	do-t	dot

Uu

pu	pu-p	pup
fu	fu-n	fun
su	su-b	sub
ru	ru-n	run
du	du-g	dug

Once a day, read and write as many groups of words as you can read comfortably. First read *down* each group. Now read these words again, this time reading *across* the page. This is a bit more difficult, and you might find yourself reading more slowly. (Also: be *sure* to check out the activities and games beginning on page 255 for review!)

dad	bet	bin	hop	bug
had	get	din	mop	hug
mad	met	fin	top	dug
sad	pet	win	lop	mug
bag	bed	did	nod	fun
nag	fed	hid	rod	bun
tag	red	rid	sod	run
sag	led	lid	pod	sun
lap	beg	nip	dot	but
nap	leg	rip	hot	hut
map	peg	tip	not	gut
gap	Meg	sip	lot	nut

The person who FOLLOWS THE CROWD usually will get NO FURTHER!

Read across the page:

tag	nag	get	pet	hug	bug
hid	lid	red	bed	hop	top
rip	tip	hot	lot	nap	lap
nut	hut	sad	dad	fun	run
beg	Meg	win	fin	nod	rod

Read down each group of words first, and then read them across the page. Try copying or writing some of these words from dictation also—perhaps about five to ten words. Writing words helps you remember them better!

bat	den	big	rum	hot
fat	hen	dig	gum	got
hat	men	pig	hum	lot
rat	pen	wig	sum	rot
Pat	ten	rig	mum	dot
dip	jug	him	ban	bet
hip	lug	Jim	fan	pet
lip	pug	dim	man	met
zip	rug	rim	pan	let
tip	tug	Tim	ran	set

Becoming educated is getting to know all of the things you DIDN'T KNOW that you DIDN'T KNOW!

Only the first letter in each phrase is different. Read across:

fat bat	ten men	big rig
hum sum	yam jam	lug jug
tan van	den pen	pig dig
tug rug	Pat hat	get jet
got hot	Sam ham	man ran

Phonics Pathways: Clear Steps to Easy Reading and Perfect Spelling **47**

Three-Letter Words Review

You may review these words either by reading them directly from the next page, or by playing *Bag the Bugs* with the cards, as directed below. (There is a master *Bag the Bugs* in the appendix if you would like to continue playing this game with other lessons.)

First read the words, then write them from dictation, using The "Short Sheet of Vowels" on page 256. (See page 5 for directions.) Just copy them if dictation is too difficult at this time. If you still have trouble writing, just trace a few of these words on the desktop with your fingertip. Reading skills frequently develop faster than writing skills, and we don't want to hold you back.

If you still need to sound out each letter individually, please read that word again. This time, blend all the letters together into *one smooth sound*. Blending skills are so important!

Bag the Bugs

(This game needs a box with a lid.)

1. Make several copies of the *Bag the Bugs* game on the opposite page on cardstock. Laminate and cut apart all of the cards.

2. Place cards facedown on the table. Students take turns drawing a card and reading the words. When a bug card turns up, a student quickly puts the card in the box and slams the top down so the bug won't "sting" him! Play until cards are gone, and all players are "safe."

3. Alternatively, students keep any bug cards that are drawn, and the player with the most bug cards after all the cards have been played is the winner.

(A master copy of *Bag the Bugs* is on page 262 if you wish to continue playing this game with other lessons.)

*Take your time, and don't worry about making a mistake.
It's not whether you stumble or fall that matters ...
What matters is that you just get up and keep on going.
Sometimes it's the last key in the bunch that opens the lock!*

bug hop	Jim hum	mad Meg	wet gum
sun hat	big man	mop van	nip Dan
fig jam	Pat run	zip bag	hot mug
beg Nan	fat pig	get cat	fed Gus
Ned jog	red jug	tip top	pup hid

The TWO SHORTEST WORDS in the English language are I and a. You simply name the letter, and THAT is the WORD!

Let's try reading "I" and "a," together with a few of the three-letter words you are now able to read. Read down each group.

By the way, "a" is what we use if the following word begins with a consonant, as in "a bug." But "an" is what we use if the next word begins with a vowel, as in "an ant," "an elf," "an igloo," "an octopus," or "an umbrella." "A" and "an" mean the same thing!

I get.
I get wet.

I had.
I had fun.

I bet.
I bet Dad.

I got.
I got jam.

I sip.
I sip pop.

I hug.
I hug Mom.

I win.
I win a van.

I pet.
I pet a pig.

I pop.
I pop a bag.

I ran.
I ran a bit.

I dug.
I dug an ant.

I sit.
I sit a lot.

hug pup	I hug a pup.
wet pup	I hug a wet pup.
big pup	I hug a big, wet pup!
fed pig	I fed a pig.
fat pig	I fed a fat pig.
big pig	I fed a big, fat pig!
met elf	I met an elf.
sad elf	I met a sad elf.
big elf	I met a big, sad elf!

jog bit	I jog a bit.
hop lot	I hop a lot.
	I jog a bit and hop a lot!
mop bit	I mop a bit.
run lot	I mop a bit and run a lot.
sip bit	I sip a bit.
sup lot	I sip a bit and sup a lot!

To AVOID that RUN-DOWN feeling ... CROSS STREETS CAREFULLY! (Read across the page.)

Pyramid (See also pages 253 and 254.)

Pyramid is an enjoyable game that will help you read sentences more easily. It bridges the gap between reading *whole words* and reading *longer sentences.* This is an excellent way to strengthen your eye tracking and increase your eye span, and besides, it is a lot of fun!

Read each line across the page, beginning with the very top word. At first, you are *not expected* to be able to read the longer sentences at the bottom of the page. In time, and with practice, you will be able to read these long sentences. (Remember to put a sheet of paper under the line you are reading, if this is helpful.)

Now try *writing* these phrases from dictation, beginning at the top, to see how many words you are able to remember at one time. Practicing this will develop your *auditory* ability to recall images sequentially, just as playing *Memory* will help develop your *visual* memory skills (see "Getting Started," page 2).

Keep practicing with *Pyramid* to develop your eye-tracking skills. It will help you be able to read the sentences in these lessons much more easily. Sooner or later you will be able to read *anything!* It just takes time and practice. There is an additional *Pyramid* exercise in the back of the book, on pages 253 and 254. Read it, as well. Pyramids are excellent "warm-ups" for all of the lessons to come!

And nowhere is there a secret of how to *quickly* enough to hold your interest *slowly* enough to experience success Everyone must find his or her have a *really good* lesson: You must proceed (otherwise you may become *bored*) but (otherwise you may become *frustrated*). very own pace ... *you find yours!*

sip

Sip pop.

Jan sips pop.

Jan sits and sips pop.

Jan sits in sun and sips pop.

Jan sits in sun and sips pop in a mug.

Jan sits in hot sun and sips pop in a big mug.

Jan sits in hot sun and sips hot pop in a big mug!

"K" is how the letter looks, and /K/ is how the letter sounds.

/K/ can be spelled in several different ways:

1. /K/ is usually spelled "k" if the following letter is "e" or "i," as in "keg" or "kid."

2. /K/ is usually spelled "c" if it is followed by any other vowel, as in "cat," "cot," or "cup."

/K/ = c-, k-

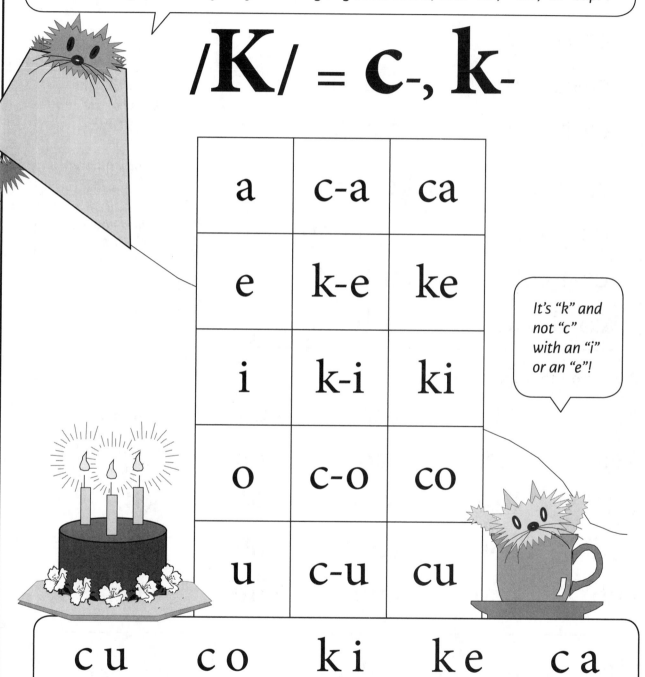

a	c-a	ca
e	k-e	ke
i	k-i	ki
o	c-o	co
u	c-u	cu

It's "k" and not "c" with an "i" or an "e"!

| cu | co | ki | ke | ca |
| ki | ca | cu | co | |

Cat, kite, cake, cup

Read down each set of words:

ca-t cat	ke-g keg
ca-n can	Ke-n Ken
ca-p cap	
ca-d cad	ki-d kid
ca-b cab	ki-ss kiss
ca-m cam	ki-t kit
co-p cop	cu-p cup
co-t cot	cu-t cut
co-d cod	cu-b cub

Read across the page:

can	cat	cap	cab	Cass
keg	Ken	cad	cup	cop
kit	kiss	Kim	kid	kill
cod	cot	con	cob	cog
cub	cud	cup	cuff	cut

Ken cup	kid Cass	cab cut
Kit can	kiss cat	cop cap

/k/ = -ck

The /k/ sound at the *end* of a short-vowel, single-syllable word is usually spelled "-ck." (See page 117 for a definition of "syllables.") Read across the page:

so-ck	sock	sa-ck	sack
ti-ck	tick	to-ck	tock
du-ck	duck	su-ck	suck
bu-ck	buck	lu-ck	luck
Ri-ck	Rick	si-ck	sick
pi-ck	pick	Ni-ck	Nick
Ja-ck	Jack	pa-ck	pack
ra-ck	rack	ro-ck	rock

We are NOT here on earth to see THROUGH one another, but to SEE ONE ANOTHER THROUGH!

Read across the page (only the *beginning letters* of the words are different):

a e i o u

rack	Jack	back	sack	hack	lack
deck	beck	peck	neck	peck	deck
pick	sick	tick	Nick	kick	lick
rock	sock	dock	hock	lock	jock
suck	tuck	luck	muck	duck	buck

pick Rick	back pack	luck suck
tuck buck	kick Nick	lack sack
mock jock	Jack back	Rick sick
lock dock	peck neck	duck muck

Phonics Pathways: Clear Steps to Easy Reading and Perfect Spelling **55**

These /k/ words are all spelled *differently*. Read across the page: (Remember to check out some of the great tips and fun games found from page 255 on!)

kiss cat	mock Rick	lick keg
pick lock	Jack can	Kip hock
duck peck	lack buck	cut sock
kick cot	pick sack	cap rack
back pack	lick cup	tick tock
lock deck	tuck neck	Kim luck
nick jock	Ken sick	suck rock

The only thing wrong with doing NOTHING is that you NEVER KNOW when you are FINISHED!

These words combine the "c-k-ck" sound with lessons previously learned:

miss Jack	get rock	kid Nan
pick fig	duck bit	fat sock
pack rug	cut sack	pig lick
tuck Don	Jack sat	lug rock
mop back	lack wig	bad luck
Kim ran	Rick hop	hug cat
kick bug	job back	tug pack
pug wag	lack nut	cup rack

/K/ = c-, k-, -ck Review

nick cup   I nick a hot cup.

lack sock   I lack a red sock.

duck peck   A duck can peck!

Ken back   Ken is back in bed.

pack sack   I can pack a big sack.

kiss sick   I kiss a sad, sick cat.

Jack back   Jack had a back deck.

kick rock   I can kick a big rock.

Review these words once a day. Read as many as you can. Now write some of them from dictation as well.

From now on copy or write about five or ten words, or three to six phrases and sentences, as an ongoing part of every lesson for the rest of this book. (At least try writing them, but if it slows you down too much, then just trace them with your fingertip for a while.)

Practice until you are able to read these words effortlessly and smoothly, and spell them correctly.

Try to do something every day, even though you may not always feel like it. Think of it this way:

A DIAMOND is nothing but a piece of COAL that MADE GOOD under PRESSURE!

Two-Consonant Endings

Now you are ready for *four-letter* words! Working from left to right, read the two-letter blend, then the three-letter blend, and finally the four-letter word. To begin with, these words will be broken down as follows. Read across the page:

$$\text{sa} \qquad \text{san} \qquad \text{san-d} \qquad \text{sand}$$

$$\text{fe} \qquad \text{fel} \qquad \text{fel-t} \qquad \text{felt}$$

You should be able to read the three-letter blend *smoothly,* add the last letter, and then read the *whole word* in *one smooth blend.* Read (and then write if you can) as many words as you are able to each day.

TEACHING TIPS: After the next two pages, these words will not be broken down as above. If some of them should be difficult to read, it can be *very* helpful to cover up the last letter with a piece of paper, read the three-letter blend, uncover the letter, and then read the whole word:

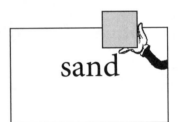

Do this as often as you need to in order to read these words smoothly. If these words continue to be difficult for you, just stay with the three-letter-word section of the book for a while to build up your reading skills until you are able to read these four-letter words a little bit more easily. Remember—there is *no hurry!*

Try reading the little "stories" in the window boxes. They contain only words made of letters that you have already learned, and are a good introduction to "real reading." If this is easy for you, it might be a good time to try some beginning phonics readers.

However, if these stories are too difficult to read just yet, then read only the words to the left of each sentence, and try to follow along with your eyes as your teacher *slowly* reads these sentences and underlines each word with his or her finger.

REMEMBER: If your eyes "skip around" while reading, hold the *Short-Vowel Stick* or a piece of paper underneath the line you are reading, or cut out a rectangle from a plain piece of paper as described on page 39. Do this for as long as you find it helpful.

THINK ABOUT IT: After you read each little story, discuss it with your teacher. Who were the characters? What happened in the story? It's important not only *to be able* to read, but *to understand* what you are reading!

There are FOUR WORDS in these stories in which the "s" sounds like "zzz": "is," "his," "as," and "has." Let's practice these words first, before we begin reading double-consonant endings. Read down each group:

is	his	is
is mad	his bed	jet is
is mad as	his bed has	his jet is
as	has	as
as hot	pup has	bad as
as hot as	his pup has	as bad as

Now let's give some four-letter words a try! Read across the page:

fe	fel	fel-t	felt
sa	san	san-d	sand

fel-t	Ben felt.
san-d	Ben felt sand.

ru	run	run-s	runs
fa	fas	fas-t	fast

run-s	Ben runs.
fas-t	Ben runs fast on sand.

ru	run	run-t	runt
he	hel	hel-d	held
te	ten	ten-t	tent

run-t	Ben has a runt pet pig.
hel-d	Ben held his pet pig, Gus.
ten-t	Gus is as fat as a big tent!

ro	rom	rom-p	romp
ju	jum	jum-p	jump
re	res	res-t	rest

rom-p	Ben and Gus romp.
jum-p	Ben and Gus run and jump.
fas-t	Ben runs fast, but Gus puffs a lot!

There's only ONE THING that SITS its way to success ... a CHICKEN!

mi	mil	mil-k	milk
lu	lum	lum-p	lump
fe	fel	fel-t	felt

mil-k	Ben and Gus sip hot milk.
lum-p	Gus has a lump in his milk.
min-t	His lump is a big, fat mint.
bes-t	Gus yells, "Mint milk is best!"

Ss

sa	sap
se	set
si	sip
so	sob
su	sum

sa	san	sand
se	sen	send

Mm

ma	man
me	met
mi	mid
mo	mop
mu	mud

mi	mis	mist
mi	mil	milk

Ll

la	lan	land
le	len	lend
li	lis	list
lo	lof	loft
lu	lum	lump
li	lim	limp

Ff

fa	fas	fast
fe	fen	fend
fi	fis	fist
fo	fon	fond
fu	fun	fund
fe	fel	felt

Ben felt	Ben felt sand.
his sand	His sand is hot.
runs fast	Ben runs fast on hot sand.

Bb

ba	ban	band
be	ben	bend
bi	bil	bilk
bo	bon	bond
bu	bus	bust
be	bes	best

Rr

ra	ram	ramp
re	res	rest
ri	rif	rift
ro	rom	romp
ru	rus	rust
ra	raf	raft

Dd

da	dam	damp
de	des	desk
di	dis	disk
du	dum	dump
de	den	dent
du	dus	dust

Hh

ha	han	hand
he	hel	held
hi	hin	hint
hu	hus	husk
hu	hun	hunt
hu	hul	hulk

KEEP your TEMPER ... nobody ELSE wants it!

Ben kept	Ben kept a pet pig.
held Gus	Ben held Gus, his pet pig.
romp hunt	Gus and Ben romp and hunt.

Gg

ga	gas	gasp
gu	gul	gulp
gu	gus	gust

Tt

ta	tas	task
te	ten	tent
tu	tus	tusk

Pp

pe	pes	pest
pu	pum	pump
pe	pen	pent

Kk

ki	kil	kilt
ke	kep	kept
ke	kel	kelp

Jj

ju	jus	just
ju	jum	jump
je	jes	jest

Ww

we	wep	wept
wi	wim	wimp
wi	win	wind

Not everyone at this point will need to read the two-letter blends first. If you still tend to reverse letters or words, then it is best that you practice your EYEROBICS by reading each blend FIRST.

jump land	Ben and Gus jump on land.
just tent	Gus is just as fat as a big tent.
jogs pants	Ben jogs and Gus pants.

-mp

ca	cam	camp
du	dum	dump
ro	rom	romp
li	lim	limp
ju	jum	jump

-nd

fe	fen	fend
ha	han	hand
re	ren	rend
be	ben	bend
me	men	mend

-st

ru	rus	rust
be	bes	best
mi	mis	mist
la	las	last
ju	jus	just

-ft

le	lef	left
ra	raf	raft
li	lif	lift
tu	tuf	tuft
gi	gif	gift

COOPERATION is spelled with TWO LETTERS: **W** *and* **E**!

Ben left	Ben left Gus on his raft.
just lump	Gus is just a big, fat lump!
ants milk	Ben fed Gus ham, jam, ants, figs, gum, and milk.

-nt

de	den	dent
re	ren	rent
mi	min	mint
ra	ran	rant
le	len	lent

-lk

si	sil	silk
mi	mil	milk
hu	hul	hulk
bu	bul	bulk
bi	bil	bilk

-lt

fe	fel	felt
be	bel	belt
me	mel	melt
hi	hil	hilt

-ld

gi	gil	gild
we	wel	weld
he	hel	held
me	mel	meld

If you point a finger at someone else, remember this ... three of your fingers are pointing back at YOURSELF!

jumps tub	Ben jumps in his hot tub.
went well	Gus went in his hot tub as well.
felt mad	Ben felt mad.
just jump	"Gus is just a pet pig. Pigs can not jump in hot tubs!"

-lf

el   elf
gul   gulf
sel   self

-lp

hel   help
gul   gulp
kel   kelp

There is NEVER *a* WRONG TIME *to do the* RIGHT THING!

-pt

op   opt
rap   rapt
wep wept
kep   kept

-sk

cas   cask
tas   task
bas   bask
tus   tusk

-sp

lis   lisp
gas   gasp
ras   rasp
wis   wisp

red bug	A big, red bug bit Gus.
tusks hump	It had big tusks and a hump.
wept help	Gus wept, "Help! Help!"
leg bump	His leg had a big, bad bump on it.
limp lump	Gus fell in a big, limp lump.
must rest	Gus must rest. His bump must mend.

Read across the page:

rom romp	jum jump	pan pant
min mint	san sand	ben bend
run runt	hin hint	mil milk
res rest	hel help	rus rust
dam damp	gul gulp	san sand
sul sulk	fel felt	len lend
hel held	tas task	sel self
sen send	mis mist	

You can't climb the ladder of SUCCESS with your HANDS in your POCKETS!

held mints	Gus held ten big mints in his hand.
romps jumps	Gus romps and jumps on hot sand.
bends damp	Gus bends and gets a damp rock.
mints sand	His big mints fell on hot sand.
gulps mints	Gus gulps ten big sand mints!
felt sulks	Gus felt sick. Gus sulks a lot.

Read DOWN each group first, by word family. It's easier. Then read ACROSS the page.

(TEACHING TIP: When you read across, put a piece of paper underneath the line you are reading to help keep you on track. Also, try reading just part of the page at a time, and/or use these words with some of the games and activities beginning on page 255.)

damp	mint	silk	lift	sent
ramp	hint	milk	sift	bent
camp	lint	bilk	gift	lent
lamp	tint		rift	dent
		bond		went
help	rest	pond	mask	rent
yelp	test	fond	task	tent
kelp	best		cask	
	vest	band		wept
felt	west	hand	pump	kept
belt	lest	land	lump	
pelt	nest	sand	bump	bust
welt	pest		jump	dust
melt		limp	dump	must
	send	wimp	hump	rust
fast	tend			just
mast	mend	runt	list	
past	lend	punt	fist	hilt
last	bend	hunt	mist	tilt
vast	fend			wilt
pant	weld	bulk	dusk	pulp
rant	held	sulk	tusk	gulp

Two-Consonant Endings Review

Only the *beginning letter* is different in each of the following phrases:

went bent	sent lent	Kent sent
camp damp	lamp ramp	vamp camp
land sand	band hand	sand band
duck luck	buck suck	tuck muck
lump bump	dump jump	pump sump
fist list	mist fist	list mist
cask mask	bask task	ask mask

lift a gift

list in fist

rest is best

melt and felt

hunt his runt

yelp and help

hand in sand

These are phrases, not sentences. That's why they don't begin with a capital letter and end with a period.

dust and rust

duck has muck

jump on bump

bend and send

wept and kept

milk is silk

tusk at dusk

Once a day, read and then write a few words on this page. Do this until you are able to read and spell them EASILY. You should be able to read these words WITHOUT having to sound out every letter. For example, if you find yourself reading "s-a-n-d" for "sand," cover up the last letter and read the three-letter blend first, "san-d," just as you did on page 58.

Continue reading words in this way until you are able to read them by blends and syllables automatically. Soon you will be able to read whole words at a glance!

Reading these sentences can be difficult, and it takes time. The games and activities in the appendix can be of great assistance here to reinforce and cement learning.

-y

A SUFFIX is an ending that is added to an existing word, that changes its use or meaning. In this section we shall learn the "-y" suffix. Remember when we learned that there are five short-vowel sounds? There is *another* letter that also can be a vowel. It is the letter "y." When "-y" is used as a suffix, it has a long "e" sound, as in the word "bunny."

NEW FEATURE: From now on, every new sound introduced for the first time will be illustrated with a sample picture and word, with the sound being learned highlighted in larger, bold print. Simply name the picture out loud, and you will hear *exactly* how to pronounce the new sound or letter. This feature will greatly ease learning how to read, and prove to be *enormously* helpful!

If a single-syllable word *already has* a double-consonant ending, just add "y":

mist   mist̸y   misty   misty

However, if the word only has *one* consonant on the end, that consonant must be *doubled* before adding the "y" in order to keep the short-vowel sound:

bun   bun̸n̸y   bunny   bunny

A single-syllable, short-vowel word must *always* have a double consonant at the end before adding any suffix beginning with a vowel. If the word does not end with a double consonant to begin with (as in "fun"), then the last consonant must be doubled before adding a suffix. Knowing these rules will really help your spelling! Read these words once a day, and then spell a few of them from dictation.

There is no secret to success except

HARD WORK!

There is only ONE PLACE where SUCCESS comes before WORK ... Can you guess where?

In the **DICTIONARY!**

Here "y" is added to words with *two-consonant* endings.

and	And-y	Andy
dust	dust-y	dusty
hand	hand-y	handy
rust	rust-y	rusty
sand	sand-y	sandy
milk	milk-y	milky

Be sure your MIND is running before you put your MOUTH in gear!

dusty and rusty	jumpy and bumpy
handy and dandy	candy is sandy
silky and milky	lumpy and dumpy
Andy is sandy	husky and dusky
ducky and lucky	dolly is jolly
hulky and bulky	pesty and testy

jumpy sick	Ben felt jumpy and sick.
pesty bug	Ben has a pesty bug.
bumpy bed	Ben rests on his bumpy bed.
Gus hid	Gus hid in Ben's bed.
lumpy bump	Gus is a fat, lumpy bump in Ben's bed!

On this page, "-y" is added to three-letter words with only *one* consonant at the end, and so we must *double* this consonant to keep the short-vowel sound:

run	run-n-y	runny
pen	pen-n-y	penny
sun	sun-n-y	sunny
Dan	Dan-n-y	Danny
fun	fun-n-y	funny
bun	bun-n-y	bunny

SEVEN DAYS without LAUGHTER MAKE ONE WEAK!

More three-word phrases to practice!

kitty is bitty	bunny is funny
Buzzy is fuzzy	Paddy has daddy
Jenny has penny	Buddy is muddy
sunny and runny	Danny has nanny
Bobby has hobby	puppy and guppy
Kenny and Benny	Kimmy and Jimmy

Jimmy fuzzy	Jimmy has a fuzzy bunny.
bunny Sammy	Jimmy's bunny is Sammy.
misty pond	Fuzzy Sammy fell in a misty pond.
funny muddy	Funny Sammy is muddy and wet!

-y Suffix Review

These phrases are more difficult because they do not rhyme:

milky candy	silly Danny
rusty dolly	jazzy Sammy
sandy bunny	funny Penny
fuzzy kitty	dusty Bobby
muddy puppy	lucky Kenny
funny nanny	peppy Buddy

misty pond	I fell in a misty pond.
funny muddy	Gus is funny and muddy.
Jenny penny	Jenny has a rusty penny.
Andy fuzzy	Andy has a fuzzy kitty.
dusty windy	It is dusty and windy.
lumpy rock	His bed is lumpy.
	His bed is as lumpy as a big, fat rock!

Review as many words as you can once a day. Read them first, and then write them.
Do this until you are able to read them SMOOTHLY and write them CORRECTLY ...
and just keep on going! Try to be like a DUCK ...
It's calm on the SURFACE, but it paddles like mad UNDERNEATH!

Twin-Consonant Endings

Here's a *neat trick* to remember that will *really help* your *spelling!* When a short vowel in a one-syllable word is followed by a final "l," "f," "s," or "z," we usually *double* the letters in order to keep the short-vowel sound. Read across the page:

tell	fell	well	sell
will	hill	fill	dill
doll	loll	bell	dell

We LOSE GROUND when we SLING MUD …

Biff	jiff	tiff	miff
buff	puff	huff	muff

bass	Cass	lass	mass
sass	Bess	mess	Tess
hiss	kiss	miss	fuss

jazz	buzz	fuzz	fizz

tell Bess	sell Puff	kiss Tess
mass mess	fell well	will tell
Jess huff	fizz hiss	puff hill
mass mess	buff doll	lass tiff
miss Puff	Cass will	Jeff fell
Bess fuss	bass jazz	sell doll

Fluency Reality Check: Real and Nonsense Words

Why on earth would anyone want to spend time reading nonsense words? It turns out that many children have strong sight memories and unconsciously memorize words, even when shown how to decode them. This habit can result in phonics skills falling by the wayside, without their even being aware of it.

Reading nonsense words is an excellent way to check whether or not phonics skills are truly embedded in your learners' strategy when reading. They should be able to read both real and nonsense words with approximately the same degree of ease, accuracy, and speed.

Below is a list of nonsense words to use as a test of phonics skills learned so far. Have your students read about six of these words out loud, and then choose six words from any previous lesson, such as those on page 68. Each group of words should be read with approximately the same ease, speed, and accuracy.

If there is a large discrepancy between the two, consider it a wake-up call! It might be wise to include nonsense words in these lessons for a few minutes each day, or go back to a particular phonics lesson that might be needed:

tas	boj	nes	pab	jid
waf	yut	gis	vem	foj
yim	pez	laj	kun	gox
heb	yaf	ses	mav	wep
ruck	pund	rab	pid	seffy
gond	belky	baft	semp	tast
rulp	hilf	vuz	tusty	jund
bock	kest	leck	ralk	rond
fosty	juck	himp	zendy	zeck

Consonant Digraph Endings

Now we are ready for something called CONSONANT DIGRAPHS.

So far, when we have had two consonants in a row, we have sounded out *each one*, as in "help." Both the "l" and the "p" are read.

Sometimes, two consonants next to each other make only *one* sound, which is different from either one. We call this a *consonant digraph*.

For example, the letters **s** plus **h** sound like /sh/. We say "*shhhhhh*" when we want someone to be quiet:

Shhhhhhhhhhhhhhhhhhhhhhhhh ...

ru-sh rush   ba-sh bash   me-sh mesh

In this section, we shall practice reading these digraphs at the *ends* of words. (Every so often there is a "sneak preview" of what these digraphs sound like when put at the *beginning* of a word. More on beginnings later.)

TEACHING TIP: When reading the words in these lessons, keep a list of the ones that are especially difficult. There are always a few! After you have read the whole group of words, go back to the difficult ones and read them again, carefully. Be sure to include them in your spelling as well—writing them out will actually help make them easier to read!

Some of you may not be quite ready to read the sentences in these lessons. Or perhaps you are able to read them, but it is difficult. Unless you are able to read them fairly easily, here is a suggestion on how to proceed:

1. *Read the two words to the left of the sentence. Have your teacher read the sentence to you while you move a finger slowly across the sentence, underneath each word. Follow the reading with your eyes, and when your teacher gets to each one of the two words you have just read, he or she will stop and let you read that word.*

2. *You and your teacher both read the same sentence TOGETHER.*

3. *Now you read the sentence YOURSELF! (If you are able to, that is. If not, do only steps one and two for a while, or even just step one.) Proceed in this manner for as many sentences in this book as you need to.*

After you read a sentence, think about what happened. Can you describe it in your own words? Try doing this with a few practice sentences on every page from now on, to be sure that you understand what you are reading. Your teacher can tell you the meanings of any words that you may not know.

-sh

ba-sh	bash		ra-sh	rash
ma-sh	mash		sa-sh	sash
da-sh	dash	fish	ga-sh	gash
ha-sh	hash		la-sh	lash
fi-sh	fish		di-sh	dish
wi-sh	wish		gu-sh	gush
hu-sh	hush		ru-sh	rush
ca-sh	cash		po-sh	posh

(sneak preview)

> sh-ip ship   sh-op shop

dash cash	posh shop	rash gash
mash bash	fish dish	gush lush
lash sash	hush mush	wish fish
rush cash	fish hash	bash mash
fish rush	ship cash	lash ship

> To ease ANOTHER'S heartache is
> to forget one's OWN!

dash cash	Let us dash and get cash. Hush!
shop ship	We can rush and shop on a ship.
wish fish	I wish I had a dish of fish hash.

-th

pa-th	path		wi-th	with
ba-th	bath		ma-th	math
ha-th	hath		pi-th	pith
Se-th	Seth		Be-th	Beth
Ka-th	Kath		do-th	doth

(sneak preview)

th-in thin	th-ump thump

path bath		with Seth
hath math		path thin
thin path		Beth thump
with math		bath Beth

When your TEMPER gets the BEST of you, it reveals the WORST in you!

Seth bath	Seth has a fish in his bath!
Beth math	Beth has a big math test.
Beth with	Beth runs with Jenny.
thin path	Beth runs with Jenny on a thin path.
thumps thin	Gus thumps a thin, red bug.

-sh, -th Review

thin fish	with cash	dash shop
Beth wish	posh bath	Beth math
dash path	Seth wish	rush path
math ship	thump dish	bath gush
with hash	rush hush	fish mushy

fish mushy	His fish is mushy.
posh bath	Seth has a posh bath!
with math	Dad helps with math.
thin fish	Gus has a thin fish.
dash path	I dash with Jan up a path.
Seth wish	Seth has a wish.
rush path	Let us rush on a path.
wish Beth	I wish Beth had cash.

Review as many of these words as you can, once a day.
Read them first, and then write them from dictation.
Continue doing this with every lesson in the book.
Take all the time you need. There is no hurry!
You are NOT running a race ...
you are learning how to READ!
And be SURE to check out the great games,
activities, and tips beginning on page 255!
(The Spelling Strategies on page 238 are also extremely
helpful if you are seriously teaching spelling at this point.)

/ch/ = -ch, -tch

This digraph can be spelled in different ways, but they are all pronounced the same way. It is usually spelled "ch" at the beginning of a word or if it follows a *consonant*:

chick

pun-ch	punch	lun-ch	lunch
ran-ch	ranch	bun-ch	bunch
pin-ch	pinch	ben-ch	bench
mun-ch	munch	hun-ch	hunch

When it follows a *vowel*, it still sounds the same but is usually spelled "tch":

pi-tch	pitch	fe-tch	fetch
ca-tch	catch	re-tch	retch
no-tch	notch	ma-tch	match
la-tch	latch	pa-tch	patch

Exceptions to this rule are: rich   such   much

Read these "-ch" and "-tch" words *very carefully!* Read across the page:

much lunch	such lunch	rich lunch
ranch lunch	hunch lunch	lunch bunch
catch latch	fetch latch	hitch latch
pitch match	catch match	fetch match
Dutch hutch	patch hutch	latch hutch

Life is not about waiting for the STORM to PASS.
It's about learning to DANCE in the RAIN!

/ch/ = -ch, -tch Review

Mitch pinch	Mitch can pinch and punch!
match catch	Can Ben match his fish catch?
fetch lunch	Mitch will fetch such a big lunch!
hunch Dutch	He has a hunch Pat is Dutch.
pitch catch	Mom can pitch and catch well.
catch fetch	Catch his cat and fetch it lunch.
fetch punch	Fetch Gus lunch and punch.
match bench	A match fell on his bench.
catch ditch	His cats catch rats in a ditch.
munch lunch	Gus and Ben munch such a rich lunch!

There's a lot of FREE CHEESE in mousetraps, but you'll never find any HAPPY MICE there ...

Hmmmmmmmm ... ?

Consonant Digraph Review

Read down first. All of the words in each column have the same *endings*. Now read across. All of the words have the same *beginnings*, but different *endings!* (**TEACHING TIP:** When you read across the page, put a sheet of paper underneath the line you are reading to help keep your place.)

mash	math	match	mask	Jack
bash	bath	batch	bask	back
wish	with			wick
	path	patch		pack
hash	hath	hatch		hack
dish		ditch	disk	Dick
mush		much	musk	muck
		Dutch	dusk	duck
hush		hutch	husk	
cash		catch	cask	

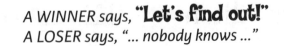

A WINNER says, **"Let's find out!"**
A LOSER says, "... nobody knows ..."

-ck	Jack is back	peck on deck
-sk	risk a disk	mask in cask
-sh	fish in dish	hush and rush
-th	Beth and Seth	math in bath
-ch	rich is much	such a lunch
-tch	hutch is Dutch	Mitch has itch

Fluency Reality Check:
Consonant Digraph Nonsense Words

It's time for another phonics fluency reality check! These nonsense words comprise consonant digraphs and other four-letter words:

setch	sesh	nusk	betch
pench	fisk	jick	hesk
lutch	binch	pusk	canch
misk	hish	pench	resh
runch	setch	sench	bisk
finchy	lusk	banchy	futchy
mesty	metchy	mechy	mesk
vusty	vutchy	vuchy	vusk

And *here* are simple sentences combining real *and* nonsense words! Do not hesitate to review the consonant digraph section as needed:

Munch a vutch.	Catch his jeth.
Ben is fenchy.	Mitch has panch.
Beth has fash.	Don is nutchy.
Jan has sunch.	Gus is pipsy.
Kitty is metchy.	Mack is lusky.
Bob has fushy.	Munch a bisky.

General Review: Short-Vowel Sounds

These phrases have mixed words, and may be difficult to read. *Take your time!*

bug is fuzzy	candy is best
test is funny	Pat has math
Beth has hunch	camp is sunny
pinch and itch	penny is cash
latch on rack	shop on ship
fetch a dish	jelly in lunch
Mitch is thin	kitty is silky
Gus is fussy	catch big fish
dash in wind	jog and jump
pack his sack	path is thin
Rick is sick	such bad luck
his buddy Jack	cat can catch
Andy is silly	catch his pitch
ditch is sandy	Jenny has milk

Some people are like WHEELBARROWS ... They work only when PUSHED, and are very easily UPSET!

-ing

s-ing	sing		r-ing	ring
p-ing	ping		w-ing	wing
k-ing	king		b-ing	bing
d-ing	ding		l-ing	ling

ring

(sneak preview)

th-ing	thing

-ang

r-ang	rang		h-ang	hang
b-ang	bang		f-ang	fang
g-ang	gang		s-ang	sang

-ung

r-ung	rung		s-ung	sung
h-ung	hung		m-ung	mung

-ong

s-ong	song		d-ong	dong

BACKBONES are better than WISHBONES!

-ng Endings Review

Read across the page:

sing	sang	song	sung
bing	bang	dong	dung
king	kong	bing	bong
long	ring	fang	hung

sing song	ding dong	King Kong
gang sang	hung rung	long song
ping pong	king sung	wing fang

EVERYONE who got where they ARE, FIRST started out from where they WERE!

ping pong	Ping pong is fun.
king sing	A king can sing well.
rung hung	I hung on a long rung.
tongs hung	His tongs hung on a rung.
King Kong	Kong Kong had long fangs.
gang wings	A bat gang has long wings.
rang sang	I rang, and I sang a long song.
Bing sang	Bing sang "Ding, Dong, Dell."

-ing Suffixes

On page 70 we learned that a suffix is an ending attached to an existing word that changes its meaning. Here is the "-ing" suffix:

fish-ing	fishing	help-ing	helping
wish-ing	wishing	dash-ing	dashing
bash-ing	bashing	limp-ing	limping
bend-ing	bending	send-ing	sending
sing-ing	singing	rush-ing	rushing

patching matching   ringing singing

packing sacking   helping yelping

sending bending   itching ditching

jumping bumping   dashing bashing

The GREATEST MISTAKE you can MAKE in life is to be CONTINUOUSLY FEARING you will MAKE ONE!

Andy rushing   Andy is rushing and dashing.

Ben helping   Ben is helping and packing.

Jan jumping   Jan is jumping and itching.

Pat singing   Pat is singing and fishing.

Gus gulping   Gus is gulping and munching a big, fat fish lunch!

-ink

s-ink	sink		p-ink	pink
l-ink	link		k-ink	kink
r-ink	rink		w-ink	wink
f-ink	fink		m-ink	mink

(sneak preview) th-ink   think

-ank

ank	sank		b-ank	bank
d-ank	dank		H-ank	Hank
r-ank	rank		t-ank	tank
y-ank	yank		l-ank	lank

(sneak preview) th-ank   thank

-unk

s-unk	sunk		b-unk	bunk
d-unk	dunk		l-unk	lunk
h-unk	hunk		j-unk	junk
p-unk	punk		g-unk	gunk

(sneak preview) ch-unk   chunk

If OBSTACLES get in your way, do as the WIND does ... WHISTLE and go AROUND THEM!

-nk Endings Review

Read across the page:

ink	sink	sinking	ink	link	linking
ank	bank	banking	ank	yank	yanking
unk	dunk	dunking	unk	bunk	bunking
ink	link	linking	ink	sink	sinking
ank	yank	yanking	ank	rank	ranking
unk	bunk	bunking	unk	junk	junking
ink	wink	winking	ink	kink	kinking

Read and write each of these words from dictation ... and then move on.

Just keep on going! Keep this in mind:

ALL progress involves SOME risk ... You can't steal SECOND BASE and keep your FOOT on FIRST!

Hank sinking	Hank is sinking fast!
pink bunk	Hank has a pink bunk.
tank sank	His tank sank in a pond.
winking Hank	Jan is winking at Hank!
hunk dunking	He is dunking a hunk of ham in his pink sink.

Simple Long-Vowel Sounds

Up to this point, we have been building words using only short-vowel sounds. Now we are ready to learn some other vowel sounds.

In this section, we shall learn the *long* sound of each vowel. In a way, these are easiest to learn of all, because the long sound of each vowel is simply its *own name!*

The diacritical mark for a long-vowel sound is a straight line over the top of the vowel.

$$\bar{A}\bar{a} \quad \bar{E}\bar{e} \quad \bar{I}\bar{i} \quad \bar{O}\bar{o} \quad \bar{U}\bar{u}$$

The way we most frequently make a word with a long vowel sound in it is to add the letter "e" to the end of a three-letter word. The "e" we have added stays silent, but it changes the *short* vowel sound in the word to a *long* vowel sound. It is often called the "MAGIC E." Here is how it works:

$$c\breve{a}n \quad can\text{-}e \quad c\bar{a}ne$$

The long-vowel diacritical mark is called a "macron," and the short-vowel diacritical mark is called a "breve." Strange but interesting names!

We shall spend the next several pages reading words with long-vowel sounds. As always, read the words first, then spell them from dictation. You probably know to do this by now without being reminded! Therefore, from now on we will not say it very often. Please remember to *read* and then *write* the words in *EACH LESSON FOR THE REST OF THIS BOOK!*

Are there ever times when you feel afraid to TRY? You're not sure that you can DO it? Guess what ... EVERYONE is!

It's ALL RIGHT to be afraid ... it's only necessary that your courage be just a LITTLE BIT BIGGER than your fear.

Courage is RESISTANCE to fear and OVERCOMING it. It is NEVER LACK of fear.

Āā

cake

Read down each set of words keep switching from short-vowel reading *across* each row first: all then the long-vowel words. Then once again. It's a lot easier now, (can, cane, etc.) If it is too difficult to sounds to long-vowel sounds, try of the short-vowel words together, try reading down each set of words isn't it?

căn	hăt	căp	măd
cāne	hāte	cāpe	māde
pan	fat	tap	gap
pane	fate	tape	gape
Sam	fad	bass	man
same	fade	base	mane
Dan	Jan	bad	ban
Dane	Jane	bade	bane

Notice how the "ck" endings change to just "k" when "e" is added:

tack	Mack	back	lack
take	make	bake	lake
Jack	rack	sack	tack
Jake	rake	sake	take

Don't always FOLLOW where a path may lead ... Sometimes go where there IS no path, and leave a TRAIL for OTHERS to follow!

Long-A Review

These words all have an /ā/ sound. Read across the page:

bake cake	Jake rake	safe gate
late date	take game	same lake
made cape	rate Jane	mate wave
name tape	ate cake	fake pane

These words combine the /ā/ sound with lessons previously learned:

best sale	fish sale	duck sale
lock gate	ranch gate	cat gate
wish cake	rich cake	pink cake
bass lake	muddy lake	misty lake
fussy Jake	catch Jake	pinch Jake

Jane made	Jane and Jake made a date cake.
ate safe	Gus ate his cake at a safe lake.
Jake lake	Jake fell in a muddy, pale lake.
take fake	Take his fake cat and name it.
makes tapes	Jane makes tapes, canes, and rakes.

Happiness does not come from what you HAVE ...
it comes from what you ARE!

Īī

10¢
dime

Proceed as you did with /ā/ for this vowels. Remember: read *across* help. *Then* read down each group!

page and for the rest of the long each group first if you should need

rĭp	hĭd	dĭn	rĭd
rīpe	hīde	dīne	rīde
kit	pin	win	dim
kite	pine	wine	dime
bit	pill	fill	mill
bite	pile	file	mile
lick	pick	Mick	hick
like	pike	Mike	hike

*PEOPLE are like TEA BAGS …
They don't know their own STRENGTH
until they're in HOT WATER!*

These words all have a long "i" sound. Read across:

dive	tide	wide	size	life	mine
wine	vine	pile	tile	wife	hike
bite	lime	five	limes	wire	tire
hide	pipe	fine	dime	nine	dimes
live	hive	Mike	files	dine	time

Long-I Review

These words combine /ī/ with words previously learned. Read across the page:

bug bite	cat bite	duck bite
ride bike	take bike	with bike
dive tide	misty tide	pick tide
fine limes	bumpy limes	suck limes
mile hike	Jack hike	sang hike
live vine	yank vine	pinch vine
pile fish	pile sand	pile lunch
song time	dunking time	funny time
like Rick	like Hank	like jumping

time hike	It is time to hike five miles.
hide five	Hide five dimes on his bike.
Mike ride	Mike will ride on a wide tire.
wife fine	His wife likes a fine hike.
likes bite	Gus likes to bite five limes.

*To treat your FACTS with IMAGINATION
is ONE THING ...
To IMAGINE your FACTS is ANOTHER!*

Oō

hŏp   cŏp   mŏp   rŏb

hōpe   cōpe   bones   mōpe   rōbe

tot   not   cod   rod

tote   note   code   rode

doll   lop   pock   jock

dole   lope   poke   joke

Do you know what the LONGEST WORD in the English language REALLY IS?
It is "SMILES." Can you guess WHY? (The answer is upside down.)

Answer: because there is a "MILE" between the first and last letters!

These words all have a long "o" sound:

rode home	lone sole	mole hole
woke doze	hope rode	mope home
moles rove	note robe	woke joke
hope dome	hole rope	lope pole
tote bone	note vote	rove home
hope joke	poke robe	cope code

Long-O Review

Whenever you find yourself working TOO HARD over the SAME KIND of sound, go back and review that lesson. It is EXPECTED that this will happen from time to time. Some lessons need more reinforcement than others—and EACH PERSON IS DIFFERENT.

Reviewing what you have already learned is not only the BEST way to be sure you really know it well—it is the ONLY way!

These words combine /ō/ with words previously learned. Read across the page:

big rope	patch rope	hang rope
neck bone	yank bone	such bone
pink robe	long robe	fetch robe
poke bug	poke Jack	poke Hank
rode fast	rode wave	rode raft
made joke	big joke	nine jokes
Ann woke	Bob woke	Gus woke
Kate hoping	Jean hoping	Mike hoping

mole pokes	A mole pokes holes in his home.
notes robe	Jill notes Jan's long, pink robe.
woke rode	Mike woke up and rode home.
tote bone	Tote a long bone on a bulky rope.
woke mopes	Gus woke. He mopes in his robe.

Uū

There are *two ways* to pronounce the long "u" sound, with a different diacritical mark for each:

These words say "yoo": **ū = /yoo/**

cube

| cŭt | mŭtt | ŭs | cŭb |
| cūte | mūte | ūse | cūbe |

| cute mule | use mule | cure mule |
| pure mute | cure cube | use cube |

These words say "oo": **ū = /oo/**

moon

| tub | luck | duck | rub |
| tube | Luke | duke | Rube |

| rude June | rule Luke | tune lute |
| Luke duke | June rule | tube tune |

*Try to do something every day, even if you're feeling LOW,
and only do a LITTLE BIT ...
Be like the SUN ... it has a SINKING SPELL
every night, but still comes back up SHINING
EVERY MORNING!*

Long-U Review

These words contain *both* types of long "u" sounds. When you *say* the word, you will *soon see which* sound *fits best!* Read across the page:

cute June	pure tune	rude mule
use tube	mute rule	cure June
pure cube	cute duke	duke lute
use lute	June mute	rude duke
cure Luke	duke use	cute mule
use tube	cute tunes	June rude

He who KICKS CONTINUOUSLY SOON LOSES his BALANCE!

use June	Use June Lake; it is pure.
tune cute	I tune a cute red van.
June tunes	June and Luke sing tunes.
duke rules	A rude duke rules back home.
use mules	We use mules to hike up bumpy hills.
Luke uses	Luke uses pure cubes in his cup.

Eē

bee

Guess what? There are multiple ways to spell /ē/, even though they have the same sound. In this section we shall learn the "ee" and "ea" spellings as well as the "magic e." ("Ee" and "ea" are actually vowel digraphs. We'll learn more about vowel digraphs later.)

Read down:

/ē/ = e—e

| her | Ev | pet | ten |
| here | Eve | Pete | teen |

Read across:

/ē/ = ee

see	seek	seen	seed
fee	feet	feed	feel
wee	weep	weed	week
bee	beet	beef	beep
Dee	deed	deep	peep
heed	heel	peek	peel

SOMETHING TO THINK ABOUT: From now on, there will often be more than one way to spell a sound, with no rules to go by at all! This shows how it would be difficult to learn how to SPELL these kinds of words at the same time that you are learning how to READ them!

In order to learn how to read as quickly as possible, it might be best to have each spelling group dictated SEPARATELY, by "family," when you write these words; and then move on to the next lesson.

Later on, you can come back to these sections for more detailed spelling lessons.

(When you do decide to teach spelling, be sure to check out "Spelling Strategies" on page 243. It is a step-by-step guide on how to teach spelling with this book.)

/ē/ = ea

Read down each group:

sea	**ea**	**tea**
sea	eat	tea
seat	east	team
seam	each	teach

bea	**lea**	**rea**
beat	leaf	read
bead	lead	real
beak	leap	rear
beam	leak	reap
beach	leach	reach

There are three kinds of people in this world ...

1. *those who **MAKE** things happen,*
2. *those who **WATCH** things happen,*
3. *and those who **WONDER** what's happening!*

ear hear	feel feet	peep cheep
team teach	see bead	deep peal
seek peak	week weed	gear here
near Dee	real peach	beast beak
reach leak	each bee	east beach

When a two-letter word ends in "e," it has a long sound:

me   be   he   we   she

feed me   she leaps   we see
be seen   be here   she eats
we reach   he means   near me
eat beets   she feeds   he seeks
treating me   teaching me   be weak

These words combine /ē/ words with lessons previously learned.
Take time to review any rules that are especially difficult. Read across:

be here   be home   be fast
see me   feed Nick   ring me
we treat   wake me   feed fish
lean beef   pure beef   rich beef
feed me   gulp treat   Dee leaps
kids leap   reach latch   reach bunk
sink beach   bunny leaps   misty beach
reach duck   fishing beach   gulping treats
teaching me   teaching math   teaching Jack

A ship in a harbor is SAFE ...   but that's NOT what ships are BUILT FOR!

Long-E Review

feed neat   We feed each neat cat beef.

she eating   She is seen eating real meat.

seek mean   We seek each mean bee on Dee.

each peals   Each bell peals near and clear.

leaps peak   He leaps on a peak near a beach.

weak peach   Feed me weak tea and a peach.

leaping each   See Pete leaping on each leaf.

Dee teaching   Dee is team teaching reading.

peeks beast   She peeks and sees a big beast.

leap each   See Gus leap and eat each bee!

weeds peaches   Gus is eating weeds, bees, peas, tea, beef, meat, and a big peach.

Always compare yourself ONLY with the progress YOU YOURSELF have made ... NEVER compare yourself with other people. After all, if only the BEST BIRDS sang, the WOODS would remain SILENT....

Read across:

ā

| cake sale | bake sale | bake cake |
| fake lake | name lake | fake name |

ē

| see beast | beach beast | see beach |
| Pete read | teach read | Pete teach |

ī

| wide dive | wife dive | wide wife |
| like Mike | bite Mike | like bite |

ō

| mope home | mole home | mole mope |
| tote note | code note | tote code |

ū

| cute June | rule June | cute rule |
| use tube | Luke tube | use Luke |

use rake	neat joke	we dive
poke cake	hide me	we vote
team teach	beast leaps	pure lake
cute deer	fake tune	make cube
five seeds	deep lake	rake weeds
ripe peach	he reads	she leaps
take bite	bake meat	cute Kate

There is a group of one-syllable words that has a long vowel sound, *without* having an "e" at the end. Read across the page:

ō

old	sold	told	gold
bold	bolt	cold	mold
hold	fold	colt	jolt
post	host	most	both
so	no	go	roll

ī

find	rind	kind	mind
tiny	hind	wild	mild

*Ideas are FUNNY THINGS ...
THEY don't work unless YOU DO!*

These words all have long-vowel sounds:

hide me	old pine	cold jolt
told Luke	so cold	find gold
no bite	roll dime	sold bike
we joke	mile toll	wild beast
so kind	both kites	mind Jane
fine mind	go home	tiny colt
fold cane	Mike host	find robe
teach colt	told Mike	hold peach
tiny beach	pile gold	both kinds

Long-Vowel Review

she read — She can read as well as Jane.

Luke takes — Luke takes a rake and weeds.

bikes home — She bikes home five miles.

each cute — Each cute mole is peeking.

hopes time — Gus hopes it is time to eat.

five bees — Five bees hide in a safe hive.

Pete pokes — Pete pokes a hole in a dike.

bites pokes — Dee bites, pokes, and mopes.

June dive — See June dive in a deep lake!

hikes miles — He hikes five miles and takes Mike's fine mules.

*Speak not SOUR words, but SWEET ...
for someone may REPEAT 'em.
But EVEN WORSE, there MAY be times
when YOU will have to EAT 'EM!
(Crabs DIG and spiders BITE ...
so do HURTFUL WORDS ... **right?**)*

Short- and Long-Vowel Mixer

Take one group of phrases at a time. These words all contain the SAME VOWEL, but it is SHORT in the first word and LONG in the second. Read DOWN each column first: all of the short-vowel words, and then all of the long-vowel words. Now read these phrases ACROSS. (Reading short- and long-vowel words together may take more time!)

ă ā

băck	gāte	Dăn	dāte	făt	cāke
Sam	came	cat	lame	sad	fate
can	make	jam	fake	ham	bake
fan	game	cash	case	math	base
sad	Jake	dad	rake	ranch	lake
pack	tape	catch	Jane	map	sale
damp	cave	lamp	base	has	date

ĭ ī

fĭsh	bīte	Kĭt	hīde	sĭt	dīke
kid	Mike	with	life	hid	dime
pick	lime	big	hike	pig	hide
his	bike	win	kite	fit	pipe
in	time	wig	mine	tin	mine
lift	tire	Rick	bite	big	tide
is	fine	fin	wide	Nick	dine

ŏ ō

lŏck	hōme	pŏp	bōne	gŏt	mōle
Don	rode	on	dome	mob	woke
top	pole	job	hope	mock	vote
not	code	rock	cone	hop	cove
pot	hole	Tod	poke	cop	joke
hot	note	Bob	doze	mop	home

ŭ ū

hŭg	Lūke	pŭp	cūte	bŭg	mūte
gulp	cube	duck	rude	lucky	June
fun	Yule	tug	mule	sun	cure

ĕ ē

wĕt	tēa	mĕt	mē	rĕd	mēat
well	deep	set	bean	ten	bees
Beth	keep	pet	seek	Meg	dear
fed	meal	led	jeep	leg	weak
beg	Dee	get	deer	Les	weep

The BROOK would lose its SONG
if we REMOVED THE ROCKS!

Short Vowels/Long Vowels

The words in these phrases combine long-vowel words without the "-e" at the end with short-vowel words. Reading across, one word in each phrase is the same:

old socks	old fish	old song
mild mint	mild duck	mild lunch
so sick	so lucky	so much
sing most	catch most	kick most
wish gold	fetch gold	lend gold
wild kitty	wild hunch	wild dash
cold bath	cold bench	cold mist

HAPPINESS is like a BUTTERFLY …
The more you CHASE it,
the more it will ELUDE you …
But if you turn your attention to OTHER THINGS,
it comes and SOFTLY SITS on your SHOULDER!

go find	Go and find a cute, tiny, old pine.
wild sold	A wild old man sold so much gold!
old cold	An old, cold lake is wild and deep.
kind mild	A kind, mild colt folds its tiny legs.
no both	No, both kids can go and find Jane.
find most	We find Luke most kind and bold.

Fluency Reality Check
Short- and Long-Vowel Nonsense Words

Here's another phonics fluency reality check using nonsense words made up of short and long vowels. Remember: short-vowel words need two consonants to keep the short-vowel sound in the word. Otherwise, it's a long-vowel sound.

feck	feek	nesk	putchy
bot	bole	papsy	dafe
motchy	fosy	fossy	leze
resk	meetch	tash	wike
dush	dake	yunch	rute
denk	goosh	lon	jate

It's fun reading sentences combining real and nonsense words! Let's try some:

metch pone	Jane hid a metch and a pone.
hesk tume	Bob had a hesk and a tume.
sug veatch	I like a veatch and five sugs.
dosk seef	At dosk Gus naps in his seef.
mips jikes	Nan mips and jikes ten figs.
baffy nisy	Jill is baffy and nisy.
gutch heshy	Jane rests in the heshy gutch.

Suffixes: Short-Vowel Words

On page 70 we learned that endings added to words are called "suffixes," and that when you add a "-y" suffix to a short-vowel word with only *one* consonant at the end, you must *double* that consonant first to keep the short-vowel sound:

fu**n**   fu**n**-**n**-y   fu**nn**y

We also learned you don't *have* to add an extra letter if the word *already ends* in two consonants:

mi**st**   mi**st**-y   mi**st**y

The *important thing to remember* is that short-vowel words must *always* end with a double consonant before adding *any* suffix beginning with a vowel. Let's try "-ing" suffixes first. Read across the page:

-ing

si**t**   si**t**-**t**-ing   si**tt**ing

hop   hop-p-ing   hopping

hop-ping	hopping	run-ning	running
kid-ding	kidding	rot-ting	rotting
set-ting	setting	bug-ging	bugging
hug-ging	hugging	sip-ping	sipping
sun-ning	sunning	tan-ning	tanning
hit-ting	hitting	lag-ging	lagging
hum-ming	humming	tap-ping	tapping

Of all the things you WEAR, your EXPRESSION is the most important!

nap	napping	kid	kidding
hop	hopping	get	getting
jog	jogging	pat	patting
let	letting	pet	petting
hug	hugging	hit	hitting
run	running	hum	humming
win	winning	sip	sipping
tug	tugging	sit	sitting

running and humming

hopping and popping

tugging and bugging

bidding and kidding

bagging and sagging

PEOPLE are much like FISH ... NEITHER would get into trouble if they kept their MOUTHS SHUT!

Mom is humming and singing a hit tune.

Gus is panting and jogging up a big hill.

Jack is sitting and sipping his mint tea.

Jan is lifting and tugging a wet fish.

I am kidding and bugging my fat cat.

The "-ed" suffixes can be pronounced in *three different ways:*

-ed = /ed/ (It is always pronounced "ed" if a word ends in "d" or "t.")

melt melted	end ended	rent rented
lift lifted	wind winded	land landed

-ed = /d/

nag nagged	hum hummed	pin pinned
jam jammed	tag tagged	rob robbed

-ed = /t/

jump jumped	mop mopped	hop hopped
kiss kissed	back backed	kick kicked

People are a lot like CARS ...
Some are best racing UP a hill,
others work best going DOWN a hill ...
And when you hear one KNOCKING all the time,
it's a sure sign that something's wrong under the HOOD!

pin pinned	tug tugged	sob sobbed
bag bagged	nag nagged	jam jammed
tap tapped	rip ripped	cap capped
lift lifted	rent rented	dim dimmed

rented and dented	lifted and sifted
nagged and bagged	bugged and tugged
hopped and popped	sipped and dipped

-er

Here are some "-er" suffixes:

hug hugger	kid kidder	win winner
set setter	tan tanner	wet wetter
sip sipper	big bigger	job jogger
run runner	hot hotter	nag nagger

jogger is wetter	runner is tanner
tipper is bigger	winner is better
nagger is hotter	mopper is sadder

SHORT-VOWEL ENDINGS REVIEW

Short-vowel words with *double-consonant* endings: (Ending *already* doubled!)

kick	kicked	kicking	kicker
pack	packed	packing	packer
kiss	kissed	kissing	kisser
rent	rented	renting	renter
jump	jumped	jumping	jumper

Short-vowel words with *single-consonant* endings: (Must double ending *first!*)

mop	mopped	mopping	mopper
rob	robbed	robbing	robber
tug	tugged	tugging	tugger
pet	petted	petting	petter
tip	tipped	tipping	tipper

Suffixes: Long-Vowel Words

Note what happens when we add these suffixes to long-vowel "magic e" words. (These words, as you have already learned, end in silent "e.") First we drop the silent "e," and then we add the suffix:

bike = bik~~e~~ + ing = bik-ing = bik**ing**

bike = bik~~e~~ + ed = bik-ed = bik**ed**

bike = bik~~e~~ + er = bik-er = bik**er**

We do *not* double the last consonant of the word because we need a *single-consonant ending* in order to keep the long-vowel sound:

poke	poking	poked	poker
doze	dozing	dozed	dozer
save	saving	saved	saver
rake	raking	raked	raker

The words in each of these phrases have the *same* long vowel:

baking and raking   baker raked

voting and hoping   voter hoped

taking and naming   taker named

joking and poking   joker poked

The words in *these* phrases each have *different* long vowels:

dining and saving   diner saved

raking and leaping   raker leaped

moping and hating   moper hated

riding and dozing   rider dozed

Suffix Spelling Chart

Short-vowel words must always have *two* consonants before adding a suffix beginning with a vowel, to keep the short-vowel sound. *Long-vowel* words need only *one*. Each pair of short- and long-vowel words listed below has almost the same spelling, except for double- or single-consonant endings before the suffix. This changes the *meaning* of the word as well as its *pronunciation*. (Reminder: spell short-vowel words "-ck" if they end with a /k/ sound.) Read across the page:

LONG VOWEL	SHORT VOWEL	LONG VOWEL	SHORT VOWEL
mōping	mŏpping	rāking	răcking
riding	ridding	baking	backing
filing	filling	liking	licking
hoping	hopping	taking	tacking
taping	tapping	stoking	stocking
pined	pinned	liked	licked
taped	tapped	hoped	hopped
baked	backed	moped	mopped
poked	pocked	caned	canned
diner	dinner	baker	backer
hoper	hopper	taker	tacker
biker	bicker	taper	tapper
filer	filler	moper	mopper

People who brag about their ancestors are like CARROTS ... the BEST PART of them is UNDERGROUND!

Phonics Pathways: Clear Steps to Easy Reading and Perfect Spelling **115**

Suffix Review: Short and Long Vowels

hoping diver	We are hoping to see a diver.
jogging runner	A jogging runner kicked a can.
baker liked	His baker liked baking cakes.
saved tasting	We saved lunch, tasting just a bit.
joker kidding	See the joker kidding and poking.
raked saved	Jan raked and saved five dimes.
landed backed	A jet landed fast and backed up.
hissed robber	Kitty hissed and bit the robber!
jogged napped	He jogged fast and then napped.
baked licked	Gus baked, licked, gulped, and munched candy. He felt sick!

Diamonds cannot be polished without a lot of RUBBING and FRICTION ... And PEOPLE cannot be PERFECTED without a lot of TRIALS and CHALLENGES!

Multisyllable Words

SYLLABLES are small parts into which long words can be divided. Each syllable contains *one* vowel sound, and *that's* how you can tell how many syllables there are in a word! When we divide long words into syllables, we *hyphenate* them—that is, we put a dash between each syllable. We *accent* the syllable that gets the most emphasis when read by putting a slanted line after it. The longest word in the world is easily read once it is broken up into syllables! First, read each syllable below:

| tic | tas | fan |

Now read these syllables in a DIFFERENT ORDER, and see what happens.
(It is something that YOU are for having come SO FAR in this book!)

| fan | tas´ | tic |

FAN-TAS-TIC!

lim´-it	limit	ex´-it	exit
vis´-it	visit	un-til´	until
tid´-bit	tidbit	tab´-let	tablet
rob´-in	robin	wag´-on	wagon
cab´-in	cabin	sub-mit´	submit
rab´-bit	rabbit	pig´-pen	pigpen
pen´-cil	pencil	him-self´	himself
in-tend´	intend	cab´-i-net	cabinet

Here is the longest word in the dictionary! Count the number of vowels, and then count the number of syllables. Are these numbers both the same?

an´-ti-dis´-es-tab´-lish-men-tar´-i-an-ism´

/k/ = -ic, -ick

We have learned that the /k/ sound at the end of single-syllable, short-vowel words is spelled "-ck." However, the /k/ sound at the end of *multisyllable,* short-vowel words is spelled with a "-c." Read across the page:

/k/ = -ic

col´-ic	colic	frol´-ic	frolic
ton´-ic	tonic	son´-ic	sonic
fran´-tic	frantic	pan´-ic	panic
man´-ic	manic	an´-tic	antic
tar´-mac	tarmac	com´-ic	comic
fan-tas´-tic	fantastic	ter-rif´-ic	terrific

Whew ...

When a suffix beginning with a vowel is added to these words, the "-c" ending is changed to "-ck." (Remember what we learned on page 53? It's 'k' and not 'c' followed by 'i' or an 'e.' Sigh ... why is spelling SO COMPLICATED?

/k/ = -ick

frol-ic	frol-ick-ed	frol-ick-ing
mim-ic	mim-ick-ed	mim-ick-ing
pic-nic	pic-nick-ed	pic-nick-ing
pan-ic	pan-ick-ed	pan-ick-ing

frol´-ic at pic´-nic	frolic at picnic
mim´-ic a com´-ic	mimic a comic
wit´-ness is fran´-tic	witness is frantic

Gus ate terrific, fantastic tidbits at his picnic!

Dividing Multisyllable Words

Are there special rules to use when dividing multisyllable words into syllables? **YES!** There certainly are. Here are a few of the main rules:

SHORT-VOWEL WORDS are divided *after* the consonant. This is called a *"closed"* division:

prof-it	cab-in	lim-it	wag-on
ex-it	rob-in	mim-ic	prod-uct

LONG-VOWEL WORDS are divided *before* the consonant. This is called an *"open"* division:

o-pen	ru-by	e-vil	ho-ly
ra-ven	pro-gram	ha-zy	mo-ment

PREFIXES are added to the *beginnings* of words and change the meaning of them. Prefixes are always kept together:

pre-pare	pre-heat	re-do	re-fresh
dis-able	dis-pose	sub-way	sub-tract

SUFFIXES are always kept together as well:

pok-ing	cur-ing	price-less	harm-less
bik-er	rid-er	play-ful	use-ful

COMPOUND WORDS (two words put together) are divided *between* the words:

base-ball	help-mate	hill-side	sun-rise
free-way	path-way	foot-step	date-book

DOUBLE CONSONANTS are hyphenated *between* two consonants:

rud-dy	fuz-zy	rab-bit	pen-cil
don-key	mud-dy	hop-ping	Hol-land

CONSONANT DIGRAPHS, however, are *always* kept together!

lunch-es	pinch-es	fish-ing	wish-ing
pitch-ing	ranch-es	bench-es	match-ing

"-LE" ENDINGS are divided one letter *before* the "-le" ending:

gob-ble	ap-ple	muf-fle	Bi-ble
nib-ble	can-dle	hob-ble	cra-dle

VOWEL COMBINATIONS are usually kept together:

seem-ed	beam-ing	steam-ing	feel-ing
fool-ish	mov-ie	bee-tle	mean-ie

VOWEL COMBINATIONS are divided *if* they are pronounced separately:

di-et	ri-ot	cru-el	ra-di-o
fu-el	du-el	ru-in	Maf-i-a

Now you know everything you've always wanted to know about dividing multisyllable words but were afraid to ask, right?

Plural, Possessive, and X

"Plural" means *more than one*. Most of the time we just add "s" to the word:

top	tops	duck	ducks
sing	sings	cat	cats
peg	pegs	hum	hums

With words ending in "-sh," "-ch," "-tch," "-z," and "-s" (also "-x," which we shall learn on the next page), the plural is formed by adding "-es." (The "es" plurals actually sound more like "ez" when spoken!)

batch	batch-es	gush	gush-es
fish	fish-es	fizz	fizz-es
inch	inch-es	kiss	kiss-es

Don't point a FINGER ... lend a HAND!

Read across the page:

cans	dishes	pans	matches
jugs	wishes	mugs	batches
kicks	bashes	licks	catches
tops	rushes	mops	fizzes
pegs	fishes	kegs	rings
racks	sacks	packs	backs
bells	quizzes	gushes	inches
kisses	catches	matches	patches
munches	bunches	pinches	punches

When we add "-s" to show *ownership* of something, we must first put an *apostrophe* at the end of the word before adding the "-s":

Jan has a cat.	It is Jan's cat.
Robin has lunch.	It is Robin's lunch.
Ben has a fish.	It is Ben's fish.

However, to show ownership in words ending with "-s," "-x," or "-z," we only need to add an apostrophe. We *pronounce* the second "s," but do not have to *write* it:

Gus has candy.	It is Gus' candy.
Max has a duck.	It is Max' duck.
Buzz has a wig.	It is Buzz' wig.

The letter "x" sounds exactly like "cks." Read across the page:

tacks	tax	lacks	lax
Bix	box	lox	fox
Max	mix	fax	Rex
ex-it	exit	ex-ist	exist

NO person is ever BORN wise or learned!

Jan's box	Bess' wig	Bill's fox
Ben's pig	Robin's chick	Kate's home
Beth's wish	ship's exit	Gus' lunch
Buzz' van	Mom's tax	Andy's bunny

Consonant Digraph Beginnings

Now we shall try putting some of the consonant digraphs we have learned at the *beginning* of a word. The vowel sounds in these lessons will be both short *and* long, so you *may* find yourself working a bit harder to read them! If you find you are working *too hard* over a sound (vowel or ending), go back and review a few words on that page to refresh your memory.

Sh-, sh-

Read across:

sh-am	sham	sh-ut	shut
sh-in	shin	sh-ed	shed
sh-ell	shell	sh-op	shop
sh-un	shun	sh-ank	shank
sh-ock	shock	Sh-elly	Shelly

shăll	shĭp	shŭn	shĕd	shŏp	shŭt
shock	shin	shun	Shelly	shot	shin
shift	shank	shag	shall	shift	shell
shut	shack	sham	shaft	shell	sham
shāve	shēep	shāle	shīne	shēet	shāde
shade	sheen	Shane	shave	sheaf	shake
sheer	sheet	shame	Shane	shape	shone

SHORT VOWEL

LONG VOWEL

*Kindness is the OIL
that takes the
FRICTION out of life!*

Phonics Pathways: Clear Steps to Easy Reading and Perfect Spelling **123**

sh- Review

hush shop   Hush, let us rush and shop!

shot shin   Dan shot his shin bone.

shame shock   Shelly felt shame and shock.

shall shank   Gus shall munch a sheep shank.

Shane shaky   Shane is in his shaky shed.

shift shine   Golden fish shift and shine.

shall shape   Shall we run and get in shape?

shift shake   Muddy land can shift and shake.

shiny shells   I shall get shiny shells to sell.

shine Shelly's   Sun will shine on Shelly's shack.

*No matter WHAT your lot in life may be ...
BUILD something on it!
(It's not where you STARTED that counts ...
What matters is where you WIND UP!)*

Ch-, ch-

Read across:

ch-ip	chip	ch-at	chat
ch-in	chin	ch-um	chum
ch-eck	check	Ch-uck	Chuck
ch-amp	champ	ch-ill	chill

ch-eek	cheek	ch-oke	choke
ch-ime	chime	ch-ase	chase
ch-ild	child	ch-eer	cheer
ch-eese	cheese	ch-eat	cheat

---

chămp chĭp	chăt chŭm	chĭll chŏp
chump chug	check chunk	chip chin
Chuck check	chop chink	check chess
chēap pēach	chāse chēese	chōke chēek
chase chime	chide peach	cheat child
cheery child	chimes cheer	chases peach

Speak well of your enemies ...
YOU MADE 'EM!

ch- Review

Chuck chunk	Chuck chops a peach chunk.
chill chugs	Chad got a chill and chugs home.
chip chunk	Chuck's gold chip is a big chunk!
chomps chops	Gus chomps on chips and chops.
check cheery	Check the cheery, chiming bells.
chess cheap	Chuck's chess set is not cheap.
chubby chum	Gus is a chubby, cheery chum.
cheer chum	Cheer up a sad chum, and chat.
Chet chugs	Chet chugs and chases Gus.
chip-munk	A wee chipmunk chits and chats.

*Take your time! Do something each day,
but don't be in a hurry ...
Sometimes the most BEAUTIFUL FLOWERS
in the garden are the ones that take
the LONGEST to GROW!*

Wh-, wh-

Here's a *new* digraph blend! We haven't seen this digraph before because it is used only at the *beginnings* of words. Read across:

wheel

wh-en	when	wh-ip	whip
wh-eel	wheel	wh-ale	whale
wh-eat	wheat	wh-ich	which
wh-ile	while	wh-ite	white

whip	whim	when	whiz
which	whisk	wheel	while
wheat	whale	white	whine

There are three words beginning with "wh-" that we must learn by sight:

who   whose   what

There are no HOPELESS SITUATIONS ...
only PEOPLE who are hopeless ABOUT them!

whine while	which wheel	white whale
whose whip	who whisks	when whip
when whale	what whiz	while whale
whisk wheat	who whines	what whim

whose white	Whose white wheel is chipped?
which whiz	Which kid is a whiz?
who white	Who chases a white whale?
whose whip	Whose kid has a white whip?
which wheel	Which white wheel is rusty?
whine while	Ann and Dot whine while eating.
which whale	Which whale is big and white?
whose what	Whose cat is whining, and what is its name?
wheat when	Gus munches white wheat when he jogs.
while white	While we had a nap, Gus ate five white cakes.

The WINNER says, "It may be difficult, but it's POSSIBLE!"
The LOSER says, "It may be possible, but it's
TOO DIFFICULT!"

Th-, th-

The digraph "th" has two sounds.

This is the "soft" sound: **/th/ = th**

th-in	thin	th-ank	thank
th-ump	thump	th-ick	thick

This is the "hard" sound: **/t̸h̸/ = th**

th-is	this	th-at	that
th-em	them	th-ose	those

Here are two sight words beginning with this sound:

the   they

TH-, TH- REVIEW

the thing	think thin	thus this
this that	than thud	thus these
they thank	thank them	this thatch
the thump	thick thatch	they think
then these	they thump	those thumps

*There are TWO WAYS of showing one's strength:
One is pushing people DOWN.
The other is pulling them UP!*

those thin	I think those thin cats need fish.
thing thumps	That thing thumps in the thatch.
thinks thick	Beth thinks this mud is thick.
Cathy the	Cathy takes the thick cake.
thuds thumps	Gus thuds and thumps when he jogs.
then thing	Then the thick thing went thud.
they thank	They thank Cathy for the help with math.
thinks these	Gus thinks he can eat these big, thick, white cakes.
this they	This time they thank those thin kids.

*NEVER be afraid to stand up for what
YOU think is RIGHT ...
People who don't take a stand on SOMETHING
often fall for ANYTHING!*

Qu-, qu-

In the English language, "q" is always followed by "u." It sounds like "k" with a "w" added to it:

qu-iz   quiz   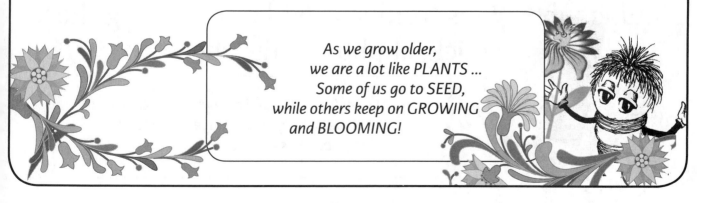   qu-ack   quack

qu-it   quit   qu-ick   quick

qu-een   queen   qu-ite   quite

qu-ote   quote   qu-ake   quake

queen

quick quake	quit quiz	quote quest
quick quote	queer quilt	queen quit
queen quacks	quest quill	queer quack

quickly quake	Run quickly, it is quite a quake!
quacks queerly	The queen duck quacks queerly.
quite quick	Dee makes quite a quick quilt.
quite queer	Gus thinks he feels quite queer.
quotes quite	He quotes quite a quick quiz.

*As we grow older,
we are a lot like PLANTS ...
Some of us go to SEED,
while others keep on GROWING
and BLOOMING!*

Consonant Digraph Beginnings Review

The words in each phrase begin with the *same* consonant digraph:

quick quake	think thin	which wheel
this thing	chit chat	shaky shack
they think	queen quits	Chuck chats
whose whip	cheer chum	ship shines

The words in these phrases begin with *different* consonant digraphs:

that quilt	check shop	quit whine
cheap wheat	they quack	shake Chet
which shop	white quilt	thank who
quick chill	what cheer	wheel chugs

those shaky   Those shaky shacks shift in a quake.

when queen   When shall the thin queen see them?

queer whale   That queer whale chased this ship!

shall grade   Chuck shall grade Chad's chess quiz.

whose chat   Whose chums chat while shopping?

quit chubby   Gus thinks he will quit chasing those quick, chubby, white sheep.

We can't go back and change our BEGINNING, but we can begin to change our ENDING ... Everybody has a FUTURE as well as a PAST!

Two-Consonant Beginnings:
bl-, fl-, pl-, cl-, gl-, sl-

Now we shall learn double-consonant *beginnings.* You will not need to read all of the vowels and blends first, unless double-consonant beginnings prove difficult. Then read *all* of the blends—*DO YOUR EYEROBICS!* Read across:

bl-

a	la	bla	black
e	le	ble	bled
i	li	bli	bliss
o	lo	blo	block
u	lu	blu	blush

> *Always THINK for YOURSELF ... or SOMEONE ELSE will do it FOR you!*

less bless	led bled	lush blush
lend blend	lock block	lack black

fl-

a	la	fla	flag
e	le	fle	fled
i	li	fli	flip
o	lo	flo	flop
u	lu	flu	flung

lag flag	lip flip	led fled
lop flop	lash flash	lap flap
log flog	lush flush	lung flung

Practicing your eyerobics will make your eyes *so* much stronger, and better able to move *smoothly* and *easily* across the page, just as aerobics will make your *body* muscles a lot stronger, so that you can *run* faster!

pl-

a	la	pla	plan
e	le	ple	plenty
i	li	pli	plink
o	lo	plo	plot
u	lu	plu	plush

SOME MINDS are like CONCRETE ... ALL MIXED UP

lug plug	lot plot	lush plush
lank plank	luck pluck	lent plenty
link plink	lane plane	lump plump

cl-

a	la	cla	clap
e	le	cle	clef
i	li	cli	cliff
o	lo	clo	clock
u	lu	clu	club

and PERMANENTLY SET!

lass class	lip clip	lap clap
lamp clamp	lock clock	lick click
luck cluck	lank clank	lump clump

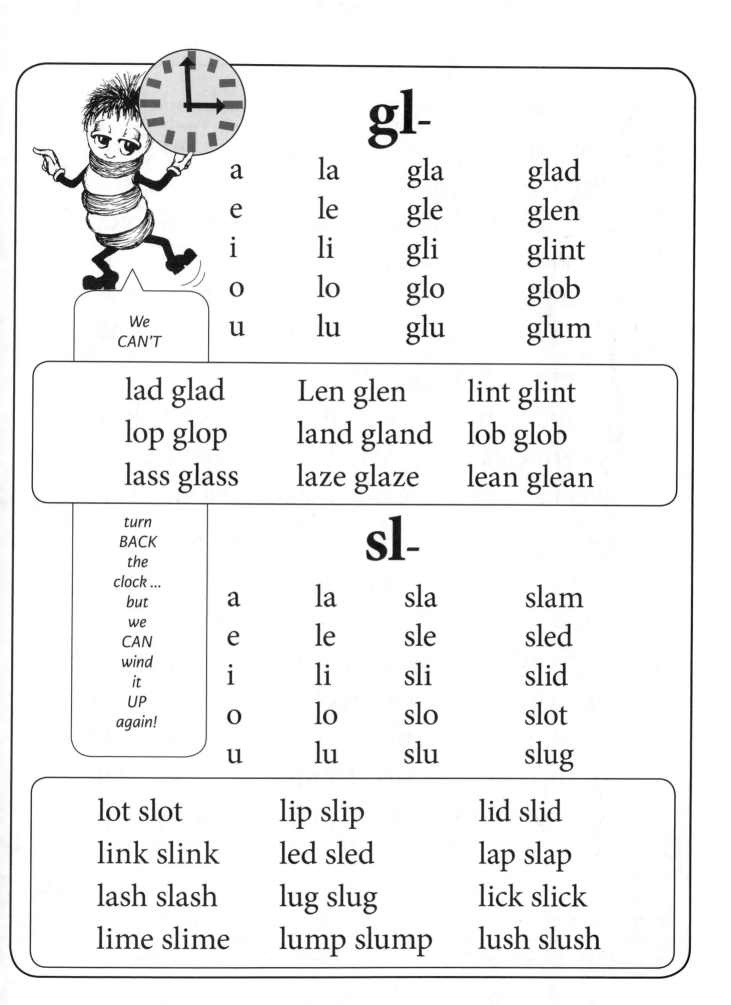

gl-

a	la	gla	glad
e	le	gle	glen
i	li	gli	glint
o	lo	glo	glob
u	lu	glu	glum

We CAN'T

lad glad	Len glen	lint glint
lop glop	land gland	lob glob
lass glass	laze glaze	lean glean

turn BACK the clock ... but we CAN wind it UP again!

sl-

a	la	sla	slam
e	le	sle	sled
i	li	sli	slid
o	lo	slo	slot
u	lu	slu	slug

lot slot	lip slip	lid slid
link slink	led sled	lap slap
lash slash	lug slug	lick slick
lime slime	lump slump	lush slush

The beginning double consonants in each phrase are *different*. Read across:

blot clot	plush slush	clap flap
flip clip	flop plop	flip slip
fling sling	flint glint	bled fled
blush flush	blink slink	clan plan
plunk clunk	glass class	slap flap
block clock	black slacks	flash slash

The long-vowel sounds in each phrase are the *same*. Read across:

blame flame	glide slide	plead sleep
gleam clean	bleak sleet	glaze plate
pleat sleeve	glade blaze	sleek fleet

The beginning double consonants in each phrase are the *same*. Read across:

blink blush	flash flag	slip slush
flip flop	plan plot	flung fleck
clip club	sled slide	clasp clock
glass glob	clung cliff	black blaze
plush plum	plump pleat	Blake bluff
slump sleep	fled flame	glum Glen
plenty plants	plush plane	slimy slug

Success is not a DOORWAY ...
it's a STAIRWAY!

bl-, fl-, pl-, cl-, gl-, sl- Review

flips flings — She flips and flings glass blocks.

slipped black — We slipped on black, slick slush.

please blot — Please blot that black ink fleck.

sled slips — His sled slips as it glides in sleet.

glad flunk — He is glad not to flunk this class.

fled flashy — Glen fled with his flashy clock.

clink clank — "Clink, clank, clunk," slid the car.

gladly plucks — Glen gladly plucks plump plums.

slip slide — I slip and slide in the slick glen.

slugs plop — Big black slugs plop on his plants.

sleepy slumps — Sleepy Gus plops and slumps into his plush, black bed.

Sometimes a good educational channel is found by clicking "OFF"!

Fun and Games

Now let's have some *fun!* You've been working hard and deserve a break. First, read these words. They *seem* to be very different but have one thing in common—they are all *palindromes.* Can you guess what that is? (Turn upside down.)

pup	eve	dad
did	sees	noon
deed	peep	toot
level	refer	madam

A palindrome is a word that reads the same backward or forward!

What is the very *longest* one-syllable word in the English language? (Answer upside down.)

Actually, there are TWO: "strengths" and "screeched."

What is the shortest word that contains *all* the vowels—a, e, i, o, u?

Sequoia!

And now, here is a sentence that *sounds like* single letters and numbers. Can you decode this "secret sentence?" (The answer is upside down.)

KT, I C U R YY 4 LC.

"Katie, I see you are too wise for Elsie."

Last, read the sentence below. Hold it upside down and look at its reflection in a mirror. Read it again. *Surprise!*

BECKIE KIDDED DIXIE

*It takes **72** muscles to FROWN and only **14** to SMILE ...
and besides, smiling adds to your "FACE" VALUE!
(If you see people without a smile, give them one of YOURS!)*

Two-Consonant Beginnings:
sm-, sn-, st-, sp-, sc-, sk-

The DARKEST HOUR is STILL only SIXTY MINUTES LONG!

sm-

a	ma	sma	smash
e	me	sme	smell
i	mi	smi	Smith
o	mo	smo	smock
u	mu	smu	smug

| mile smile | mock smock | mug smug |
| mash smash | Mack smack | mite smite |

sn-

a	na	sna	snap
e	ne	sne	snell
i	ni	sni	snip
o	no	sno	snob
u	nu	snu	snuff

| nap snap | nub snub | nip snip |
| nag snag | Nell snell | nob snob |

SPECIAL NOTE to students still reversing letters, or finding it hard to read: please begin every lesson from now on by going back to one of the pages in this section and reading across one group of words, from the vowel to the whole word. It will be a GREAT eyerobic warm up!

st-

a	ta	sta	stack
e	te	ste	stem
i	ti	sti	stick
o	to	sto	stop
u	tu	stu	stuck

tab stab	tiff stiff	top stop
tack stack	tan Stan	take stake
tuck stuck	tick stick	tock stock

sp-

a	pa	spa	span
e	pe	spe	spell
i	pi	spi	spill
o	po	spo	spot
u	pu	spu	spun

pat spat	pit spit	pot spot
pill spill	pan span	pine spine
pun spun	poke spoke	peak speak

sc-, sk-

Do you remember when we learned (on page 53) that the /k/ sound is spelled with a "k" when it comes before "e" or "i," and with a "c" when it comes before an "a," "o," or "u"?

The same thing usually happens when you put an "s" before the "k":

a	ca	sca	scat
e	ke	ske	sketch
i	ki	ski	skip
o	co	sco	Scotch
u	cu	scu	scum

The most BEAUTIFUL TREES in the world FIRST began covered with DIRT, but they ROSE ABOVE it ... GROW where you are PLANTED!

cat scat	kin skin	kit skit
kid skid	Kip skip	cab scab
can scan	Kate skate	kill skill
cope scope	cone scone	cuff scuff

smug Smith	smell smoke	smash smock
smoky smell	smear smock	Smith smile
sneaky snake	snake sneeze	snip snag
sniff snack	snatch sneak	snob snubs
stiff stems	stick stuck	stand still
stove steams	stone stack	steel stake
spill spot	speed spin	spank spine
spade spike	speak spell	spoke spend
scab skin	skunk skids	scuff scalp
scale scope	skate skids	skip skim

I do reveal the WAY that I FEEL
by the things that I SAY and DO ...
By CHANGING the things that I SAY and DO
I can CHANGE the way that I FEEL!

stiff spine	smell stale	skate skids
snatch snack	skid stone	snake slides
sneaky snob	skip stack	smug smile
sneeze smoke	stove spills	Scott sniffs
Smith speaks	stand speech	smelly skunk

sm-, sn-, st-, sp-, sc-, sk- Review

sneeze smell	I sneeze when I smell smoke.
smug fleas	Smug fleas sneak and stab Skip.
sneaky snakes	Sneaky snakes skid and stop.
stiff snobs	The stiff snobs sniff and snuff.
spilled stink	Spilled eggs stink and smell.
Spot snoops	Spot snoops, sniffs, and snuffs.
snatch stack	Snatch that stack of stiff sticks.
sticky spill	The sticky spill left a black spot.
step spin	We step, spin, skip, and skid!
stop smug	Stop that smug sneak. Scat!
spunky stands	Spunky Spot stands still.
stacks sticky	Gus smells stacks and stacks of sticky scones. Snack time!

In LIFE, as in RESTAURANTS, we must sometimes swallow things we DON'T LIKE ... just because it COMES ON THE PLATE!

br-, cr-, dr-, fr-, gr-, pr-, tr-

Read down each column:

br-	cr-	dr-	fr-	gr-	pr-	tr-
ra	ra	ra	ra	ra	ra	ra
bra	cra	dra	fra	gra	pra	tra
brat	crab	drag	Fran	Grant	pram	tram
re	re	re	re	re	re	re
bre	cre	dre	fre	gre	pre	tre
Brett	crest	dress	fresh	Greg	press	trend
ri	ri	ri	ri	ri	ri	ri
bri	cri	dri	fri	gri	pri	tri
brick	crib	drip	frisk	grip	print	trim
ro	ro	ro	ro	ro	ro	ro
bro	cro	dro	fro	gro	pro	tro
Bron	crop	drop	frock	groggy	prop	trot
ru	ru	ru	ru	ru	ru	ru
bru	cru	dru	fru	gru	pru	tru
brush	crush	drum	frump	grump	prūne	truck

FORGIVENESS is like MAGIC ...
It COOLS the hurt, but it WARMS the heart!

The words in each phrase have the *same* vowel sound. Read across:

drag pram	Fred frets	drop crock
grip slip	crank prank	crush truck
brush crust	grab crab	cram tram
press dress	drop slop	Fran tracks
trick stick	free cream	frame grate
trade crate	green creek	bride pride

The words in these phrases have *different* vowel sounds. Read across:

pram slips	frisky Grant	Fred trips
crabby Greg	Trixie drags	trim brush
Fran drops	crank crib	trick Frank
Trudy grabs	cranky Brad	grassy crest
fresh crock	crunch brick	prop truck
cliff cracks	drop crutch	grim brink
trade drinks	crave brunch	brave Grant
green grape	dream bride	free prune
crate broke	prime grade	creek froze

I hope you're remembering to review the words in each lesson until you are able to read and write them easily. If you make a mistake, try again and just keep going ... Remember ... NOBODY'S PERFECT. (That's why PENCILS have ERASERS!)

The words in each phrase have the *same* short vowel and ending. Read across:

truck stuck	grab crab	fling sling
flop plop	trip grip	black snack
cramp clamp	flap trap	press dress
track crack	slick trick	stock clock
smug slug	fled sled	slink plink
smash flash	snip drip	flick brick

The words in these phrases have *different* short vowels and endings:

sled spins	crush bricks	smack slug
scuff slacks	pluck crop	grumpy Fred
Grant frets	skip class	black flash

The words in each phrase have the *same* long vowel and ending:

grope slope	grime slime	steer clear
steam cream	Clive drive	troll stole
blame frame	clone stone	dream cream
drapes grapes	blaze glaze	bride glide

The words in these phrases have *different* vowels and endings:

smug bride	glass clean	fresh cream
crunch stone	speed skate	Grant sleepy
trust Jane	brush frame	blame trick

Beware the TONGUE ... it's very WET and likely to SLIP!

Two-Consonant Beginning Review

Here are *two* pages of review! Notice that the sentences on the next page are longer. Take it easy—you don't have to read them quickly. These sentences are more complicated, so don't get discouraged if you do slow down a bit when reading them. Everyone does. However, if you are having *too* difficult a time reading them, go back to reading them as suggested on page 76. It is important that you always feel *challenged*—but never *frustrated!*

(Remember to check out the games and activities beginning on page 255—they're a great way to reinforce learning and make it fun at the same time!)

crabby Greg   Crabby Greg drags and frets.

Brent drinks   Brent drinks milk in the grass.

trucks crunch   Trucks drop and crunch bricks.

fresh frock   A fresh frock is a dream dress.

Frank grumpy   Frank is grumpy and groggy.

Grant crave   Grant and Fred crave brunch.

Fran crutches   Fran drops the broken crutches.

Trixie frisky   Trixie is frisky and trots, but trips.

The BEST VITAMIN
for MAKING FRIENDS
is
B-1.

snake glides	The sneaky snake slides and glides on the slick path.
trip grab	I trip and grab the brink of the grim cliff.
sticky slinky	Smash this sticky, slinky, green slug. It clings!
grabs Grant's	Fred grabs Grant's frisky, tricky, black ducks.
crabby groggy	Frank is crabby and groggy, and slumps into bed.
flung branch	Greg flung the branch in a clump of green grass.
glide swift	We glide, slip, and slide with these swift skates.
sniffs brunch	Gus sniffs brunch and drops his glass of fresh milk.
grumpy cranky	Brent and Trudy trick grumpy, cranky Brad. He frets.

WHEW ... glad THAT's done!

r-Modified Vowels: /är/

So far, we have learned about the two sounds vowels usually make: the short sound, as in "rat," and the long sound, as in "rate." When a vowel is followed by the letter "r," it makes *another* sound, which has been modified, or changed, by the letter "r."

/är/ = ar

This is the diacritical mark for an "r-" modified "a" sound. It is called an "umlaut." Read down:

ark	art	card	are
bark	cart	hard	arm
dark	part	yard	harm
lark	tart	lard	charm
mark	dart	chard	yarn
park	mart	carp	barn
spark	start	harp	parch
shark	chart	tarp	farm
Clark	smart	sharp	farm-yard

yarn art	arms are	part lard
hard part	dark park	barn farm
smart carp	start harp	mark tarp
card shark	Mark bark	chard tart
lark charm	chart dart	cart spark
Clark's ark	shark harm	sharp yard

FORGIVE and FORGET! SOUR GRAPES make BAD WINE.

/ôr/ = or, ar, oor, ore, our, oar

The diacritical mark for an r-modified
There are *six different spellings* of this

4
four

"o" sound is called a "circumflex."
sound! Read down the page:

/ôr/ = or

or	cord	sort	worn
for	corn	sport	torn
fork	scorn	short	horn
pork	porch	snort	born
cork	torch	form	morn
stork	north	storm	doc-tor

/ôr/ = ar

("Ar" sounds like "ôr" when it follows a "w.")

war	ward	wart	warm
award	warn	warp	warm-up

Take a lesson from MOSQUITOS ...
They never sit around WAITING
for an opening ...
THEY MAKE ONE!

worn horn	fork pork	torn cork
short stork	warm sport	war story
sort award	short war	born morn
storm north	snort forth	warn dorm
warp form	scorn glory	wart doctor
short warm-up	torch scorch	warm porch

/ôr/ = oor

floor   floor-ing   door   in-door

/ôr/ = ore

core   tore   store   score
more   lore   shore   bore

/ôr/ = our

four   pour   course   fourth

/ôr/ = oar

oar   board   roar   soar

Here is a sentence using ALL SIX spelling patterns for the /ôr/ sound:

Four more warm storks soar indoors.

Copy this sentence on paper, and circle each spelling pattern.
Check to be sure you found them all. (It might also be fun to try writing
your OWN sentence, choosing your words from each spelling pattern!)

door horn	court Dor	for store
pour more	north lore	short oar
four doors	worn floor	corn core
soar shore	roar snort	store door
floor board	tore board	dorm floor
coarse pork	wore more	fourth torch
warm storm	porch floor	short course

/är/ and /ôr/ Review

warm for	Gus eats chard, carp, pork, corn, and warm shark for lunch.
more chores	Robin has four more hard chores she must start.
horns awards	The four horns are for Mark, and more awards are for Clark.
doctor snores	The old doctor sits on his warm porch and snores and snores.
doors warped	The four doors in the dark barn are warped and torn.
course start	Of course she can take four more courses and start sports.
horse snorts	His horse snorts and roars at the short stork in the yard.
warn sharks	Warn Clark that four smart sharks tore his floor board.

To really appreciate the dignity and beauty of an OLD FACE, you have to READ BETWEEN THE LINES!

/ʉr/ = er, ir, ur, or, ear

Here are all of the spellings for the "r-" modified "u" sound. The diacritical mark for this sound is "ʉr." If you look up "her" in the dictionary, for example, it shows the pronunciation as "hur." Read down:

bird

/ʉr/ = er	/ʉr/ = ir	/ʉr/ = ur
her	sir	urn
herd	stir	turn
pert	fir	burn
Bert	bird	hurt
jerk	birth	fur
term	mirth	cur
berth	girl	curl
Herb	dirt	curb
clerk	firm	purr
fern	first	lurk
perch	thirst-y	murk-y

It's what you learn AFTER you KNOW IT ALL that COUNTS!

curb dirt	her turn	burn fir
fur herd	hurt fern	jerk urn
Sir Herb	turn berth	pert cur
first birth	murky fir	Bert lurk
Bert purr	bird perch	firm curl
thirsty girl	firm mirth	girl clerk

Here are two more spelling patterns for this sound. "Or" sounds like /ur/ whenever it has a "w" in front of it. Read across the page:

/ur/ = or

work	word	worm
worst	worth	wor-ship
world	worse	wors-en
worm-y	worth-y	wor-sted

/ur/ = ear

earn	learn	yearn
heard	search	earth

Here is a sentence using all five of the /ur/ spelling patterns:

Bert's earth-worms stir and turn.

Copy this sentence, and circle each one of the /ur/ spelling patterns. Now try writing a different sentence, choosing your own words from as many of these groups as you can think of.

ER, IR, UR, OR, EAR = /UR/ REVIEW

her work	Herb hurt	earn fur
girl turn	her word	Gert purr
early bird	dirty worm	first work
earth first	learn work	girl heard
worst burn	worthy urn	jerk perch
search world	thirsty fern	worm curl
worthy search	perfect pearl	burn worsen

Here is a review of all the /ur/ spelling patterns. They can be tricky to learn, and it's good to take time to know them. Read down each spelling group:

er	**ir**	**ur**	**or**	**ear**
her	sir	urn	work	earn
herd	stir	turn	worth	learn
pert	fir	burn	worm	earth
Bert	bird	hurt	world	heard
jerk	birth	fur	word	pearl
term	first	cur	worst	ear-ly
fern	girl	curl	worth	search
Herb	dirt	curb	wor-ry	searched
clerk	firm	purr	worth-y	search-er
per-fect	birth-day	pur-ple	work-er	learn-er

her turn	firm dirt	girl learn
world search	earn pearl	pert Herb
hurt cur	perfect fern	Bert purr
first birth	early bird	worthy fir
worst herd	firm earth	Herb clerk
earthworm	girl worry	heard bird
jerk urn	curb dirt	worm curl
clerk learn	worker heard	searcher burn

Sometimes people are lonely because they build WALLS instead of BRIDGES.

Let's try reading some multisyllable words again, just as we did on page 117. We'll also incorporate some of the r-modified vowels we have just learned. It's fun to "build" words from "blocks" of syllables! Read down each group:

hard	sharp	art
hard-en	sharp-en	ar-tist
hard´-en-er	sharp´-en-er	ar-tis´-tic
car	form	su
car-pen	per-form	su-per
car´-pen-ter	per-form´-er	su´-per-man
or	croc	al
or-na	croc-o	al-li
or´-na-ment	croc´-o-dile	al´-li-ga-tor

hardener	sharpener	artistic
carpenter	performer	superman
ornament	crocodile	alligator

See you later, alligator …
after a while, crocodile!

If you find it difficult to read the longer words, try covering up most of each word first, and then SLOWLY move the paper over while you read each syllable. Some people find this helpful. What do YOU think? … And, by the way, don't just WAIT for your ship to come in … SWIM OUT TO IT!

/ʉr/ = er, ir, ur, or, ear Review

search stirs   We search for our pert kitty, Pearl. She stirs and purrs.

heard perfect   I heard that her work is perfect. She learns and earns a lot.

yearns world   The girl yearns and searches for peace in her world.

earth-worms   Bert heard that Herb will search early for his earthworms.

thirsty berth   Thirsty Gert curls and turns in her firm berth.

first learns   First, Gus learns to stir and turn his beef. It burns!

Fern's dirty   We must first clean Fern's dirty but pert bird.

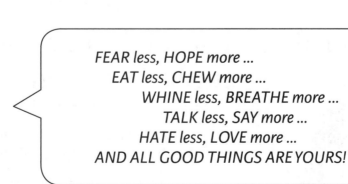

FEAR less, HOPE more …
EAT less, CHEW more …
WHINE less, BREATHE more …
TALK less, SAY more …
HATE less, LOVE more …
AND ALL GOOD THINGS ARE YOURS!

r-Modified Vowels Review

The words in each phrase have the *same* r-modified vowel sound:

Mark park	Bert purr	born morn
girl earn	hard part	larks are
worst dirt	more corn	farm yard
learn work	start harp	horn worn
award store	firm perch	four forks
worm curl	chart shark	thirsty fern

The words in these phrases have *different* r-modified vowel sounds:

Bert roar	arm hurt	sort pearls
torch burn	pork tart	Gert charm
smart bird	girl born	store pearls
worst dorm	shark curl	more chard
Clark learn	north star	warm perch
search park	dark porch	murky morn

learned four — Pearl learned that four ferns in the yard got torn in the storm.

part morning — Part of the burn on Herb's arm turned worse in the morning.

> *You have TWO EARS and only ONE MOUTH ...*
> *LISTEN TWICE as much as you TALK!*

Long-Vowel Digraphs

This section of the book will introduce some other ways to spell long-vowel sounds. We will be learning the *long-vowel digraphs.*

A digraph, as you remember, is two letters that make one sound. We have studied consonant digraphs, such as /sh/ and /th/, and we have also learned two long-vowel digraphs: /ee/ and /ea/. Now we shall learn the *rest* of them!

It may take a while to learn how to read and spell these digraphs, so remember to take *all the time you need* with each one. Also remember that when there are so many different ways to spell a sound, at first it might be best to dictate these words by *family,* as presented on page 66. They will be easier to read and spell this way.

Eventually you must be able to read and write these words randomly, in any sentence. Being able to *read* these words is the most important thing for now—you can come back to this book for more detailed spelling lessons later. (When you *are* ready to teach spelling, however, do check out "Spelling Strategies" on page 243. It's an easy, step-by-step guide on exactly how to teach spelling with *Phonics Pathways.*)

As in the last section, the review sentences are longer and use more multisyllable words. It is quite *natural* if you temporarily slow down a little bit when you read them. You are stretching and expanding your reading skills!

There *is one thing* you should watch for. If you find yourself really stumbling over the *same kind* of sounds, then you need to go back to that section of the book and take time out to review it. It is common for this to happen, and it is the *true test* of whether or not you know these rules well enough for them to be automatic when reading them. It does not matter if you are just *slowed down*—speed comes with practice—but you should not have to *struggle* with each individual word. It's very important to work at a *challenging* but *comfortable* pace!

TEACHING TIPS: Those who are still struggling with eye tracking might prefer to continue reading these sentences using the method shown on page 75. And *please* remember to do your eyerobic warm-ups if it *is* difficult for you! (You didn't forget what they *are,* did you? See page 133!)

Remember to incorporate the activities and games in the appendix (from page 255). They will reinforce learning and make it *so* much more *enjoyable* at the same time!

Why not start a NEW DIET?
No more EATING your own words,
SWALLOWING your pride,
or putting your FOOT in your mouth!

/ā/ = ai

The long-vowel "ai" and "ay" digraphs sound like /ā/. Here are some "ai" words:

aid	rain	ail	wait
maid	main	bail	bait
paid	gain	jail	trait
raid	vain	sail	faint
laid	pain	nail	saint
braid	Spain	pail	paint
aim	brain	Gail	taint
maim	drain	fail	stain
claim	train	frail	chain
plain	strain	trail	com-plaint

wait jail	laid rail	aid raid
paid maid	maim nail	pain strain
aim bait	stain rain	vain Gail
Gail braid	plain chain	sail Spain
saint faint	brain drain	frail trail
paint pail	main train	claim gain

Keep your FACE to the SUNSHINE, and you will NEVER SEE the SHADOWS!

/ā/ = ay

/ā/ is spelled "ay" when it appears at the *end* of a word. Read down:

Jay	lay	way	ray
may	play	sway	pray
say	clay	a-way	gray
stay	slay	way-side	tray
tray	flay	mid-way	fray
stray	de-lay	day	bray
to-day	lay-er	day-time	hay
cray-fish	lay-a-way	hol-i-day	hay-stack

> *Test your STRENGTH by lifting a HEAVY WEIGHT off someone's shoulders!*

gray day	Kay may	play clay
pay today	Ray betray	tray sway
spray hay	stray crayfish	May holiday

/Ā/ = AI, AY REVIEW

pray	rain	mail	train	hay	grain
play	clay	pay	maid	frail	Kay
slay	tail	pail	sway	say	Spain
main	trail	spray	paint	gray	day
aid	crayfish	wait	haystack	stay	holiday

/ā/ = ai, ay Review

Gail frail   Gail is frail and must not play on a rainy day.

mail train   The mail train is running late. Shall we wait at the gate?

tray crayfish   Gus laid his tray with crayfish on the main table today.

pay plain   Say, who can I pay for this plain, gray cake tray?

Kay lays   Kay lays chains and nails in the pail on the clay trail.

paint gray   Please paint this ship plain gray. We will wait and sail later.

Gail stay   Gail can stay late. May we play with clay while waiting?

trail freeway   Wait! I see the main trail faintly near the freeway.

LAUGHTER is a tranquilizer with NO SIDE EFFECTS!

/ē/ = ie, i, -ies

Sometimes the "ie" digraph sounds like /ē/. (We have already had the "ee" and "ea" digraphs.) "i" and "y" are not digraphs, but are included here because they both have this sound. Read down the page:

/ē/ = ie

thief	pier	field
chief	tier	yield
grief	grieve	shield
brief	re-lieve	Ka-tie
fiend	be-lieve	Las-sie
fierce	re-trieve	Con-nie
pierce	a-chieve	Deb-bie

/ē/ = i   marine   machine

We have already had "-y" endings on page 73. When we make a word with a "-y" ending plural (more than one), we must first change the "y" to "i," and then add "-es."

/ē/ = -ies

pan-sy	pan-sies	du-ty	du-ties
ru-by	ru-bies	pen-ny	pen-nies
par-ty	par-ties	ba-by	ba-bies
car-ry	car-ries	hur-ry	hur-ries
pup-py	pup-pies	kit-ty	kit-ties

/ē/ = ie, i; /-y/ = -ies Review

thief quickly	grieve kitty
chief armies	relieve Katie
shield puppy	achieve duty
carry pansies	fiend hurries
believe priest	Debbie slowly
Connie parties	Lassie's babies
marine achieves	pennies machine

Katie briefly	Katie and Debbie run briefly in the field of pansies.
puppies shield	Ten puppies hurry and shield baby Jackie.
believe marine	I believe the chief marine will be funny and brief.
carries tiers	Gus carries a party cake with cherries and ten tiers.
hand-ker-chief	Katie forgot her handkerchief. She quickly retrieved it.

The person who makes NO MISTAKES usually does not make ANYTHING!

Here "ie," "ui," and "uy" have an /ī/ sound. "y" is not a digraph but is included here because it has the /ī/ sound. Read across the page:

/ī/ = ie, y

try tries	dry dries	fry fries
fly flies	cry cries	sky skies

lie	pie	tie	die
my	by	spy	shy
why	rye	eye	Clyde
type	typ-ist	style	styl-ish
ty-coon	ty-rant	ply	ply-wood
dy-nam-ic			dy-na-mo

/ī/ = uy

guy	buy
buyer	

/ī/ = ui

guile			beguile
guise	guide		disguise

To handle YOURSELF, use your HEAD ... To handle OTHERS, use your HEART!

try pie	shy guy	rye pies
tie die	my eye	fly skies
spy tries	buyer lies	guide Clyde
by typist	my typing	spies crying
disguise eyes	stylish guy	buy plywood

/ī/ = ie, y, uy, ui Review

why Clyde	Why did Clyde cry? He tried lying.
tried eyes	She tried flying the kite by my eyes.
guide flies	Guide my fine jet as it flies with style in the wild sky.
cried pies	Gus cried and cried while his fried rye pies dried.
try disguise	Why did Clyde try buying my spy disguise?
sly guy	The sly guy tried spying by my vine.
typist buys	My shy typist buys stylish ties.
die crying	Why did Clyde's fine, shy kitten die? He is crying.
tycoon fries	The shy tycoon cried as he spilled French fries on his tie-dyed pants.

TWO PEOPLE looked at a rose bush:
One was ANGRY because the ROSES had THORNS,
the other was HAPPY because the THORNS had ROSES!

These vowel digraphs all sound like /ō/. Read down each column:

/ō/ = **oa**	/ō/ = **oe**	/ō/ = **ow**
oat	toe	own
boat	hoe	bow
goat	foe	bowl
load	Joe	low
loaf	goes	slow
road	hoes	flow
roast	Joe's	grow

hol-low	yel-low	pil-low	win-dow
fol-low	fel-low	wil-low	shad-ow

toast loaf	row boat
Joe's goat	roast oats
crow goes	coast road
soap floats	load bowl
toad croaks	yellow hoe
low shadow	fellow goes
hollow float	foam pillow
Joan follows	bowl slowly
willow blows	show window

FAITH is what helps us live between the TRAPEZES!

/ō/ = oa, oe, ow Review

boasts shows · Joan boasts and shows her load of yellow bows.

loaf float · We like to loaf, float, and lie low in Joe's hollow boat.

flows slowly · This low river flows slowly until it goes by the coast road.

willow blow · These willow trees blow in the snow and grow slowly.

follows grown · Joan follows Joe's grown goat. It goes most slowly.

show toad · Show Moe the old toad croaking on my yellow pillow!

roast loaf · Gus likes roast meat loaf, toast, and oats in a bowl for lunch.

> *Sometimes we change, not because we see the LIGHT, but because we feel the HEAT!*

There are *eight different ways* to spell /ū/ digraphs! Read down each column:

/o͞o/ = oo

too (Means "also" or "extremely.")
soon
spoon
tooth
goof
stoop
moose
moon
fool
food
choose
proof
smooth
zoom

/o͞o/ = oe

canoe
shoe

/o͞o/ = ew

new
dew
grew
drew
stew
strew
Lew
flew
blew
news
chew

/yo͞o/ = ew

few
mew
new
skew

/o͞o/ = ue

true
glue
blue
flue
Sue
due

/o͞o/ = ui

Sometimes /ū/ is spelled "ui":

fruit
fruit-cake
juice
bruise
cruise
suit
suit-able
suit-case

/o͞o/ = ou

Here are a few /ū/ words that are spelled "ou." Read across the page:

| you | youth | your | un-couth |
| soup | pouf | group | mousse |

/ōo/ = o

And finally, sometimes "o" can sound like /ū/:

do	to (Indicates "action" or "direction.")	two* (Indicates "number." "W" is silent.)
prove	im-prove	whom
move	movie	move-ment

*Note special spelling of the number "two."

Here is a sentence using *all eight* of the spelling patterns for /ōo/:

Your two moose soon chew fruit in the blue canoe.

Copy this sentence and circle each one of these spelling patterns. Now write your own sentence, using as many /ōo/ spelling patterns as you can think of.

The words in each phrase have the same /ōo/ spelling. Read across:

soon moon	Sue due	youth group
blue shoe	to prove	fool drool
Lew grew	news flew	fruit juice
loose tooth	goof proof	smooth soup
chew stew	cruise suits	do im-prove
tooth drool	Lew flew	do move-ment
moose stoop	zoom canoe	bruise suit-case
improve movie	choose spoon	suit-able cruise

NO dream comes true until you WAKE UP and GO TO WORK!

/o͞o/ = oo, ew, ue, ui, oe, ou, o; /yo͞o/ = ew Review

two suits	fool Lew	too few
goof proof	new suit	to cruise
two moose	to movie	Lew drew
chew fruit	do choose	new tooth
bruise fruit	crew flew	blue moon
choose shoe	soon stew	brew juice
few moose	Luke drew	blue spoon
youth group	Sue prove	drool soup
smooth food	move stool	bruise two

two moose	Two big moose soon grew blue under the new moon.
Sue drools	Baby Sue drools soup and soon has goo on her new shoe.
snoop blue	A goose stooped to snoop by the blue canoe and then flew.
smooth fruit	The smooth fruit juice is too cool on Lew's loose tooth.
chooses cruise	Gus chooses a cruise with food to chew and a movie, too.

Sometimes we HAVE to take a big step ...
We can't cross a chasm in TWO SMALL JUMPS!

Long-Vowel Digraph Review

The long-vowel digraphs in each group of words have the same sound. Read across:

wait train	play clay	rain today
spray grain	paint tray	gray trail
frail Kay	plain pail	bait snail
shield penny	carry babies	marine yield
believe Lassie	Debbie's grief	kitty hurries
Connie carries	shield puppies	Katie's party
buy pies	tried typing	guide Clyde
spies lied	rye dries	tried fries
why cry	my plywood	flying skies
follow goat	tow boat	hold toe
yellow pillow	willow grow	soak road
Joe's shadow	flow slowly	load boat
blue moon	chew fruit	move soup
smooth juice	moose soup	Sue prove
youth snoop	group cruise	grew tooth

a
e
i
o
u

These words contain a *variety* of long-vowel digraphs. Read across the page:

fool spies	juice stain	Joe flew
Lassie tried	chief typist	buy pail
babies grow	choose paint	rain today
marine guide	frail puppies	blue moose
pansies blow	disguise Debbie	show movie

On page 53 we learned that /k/ is spelled with a "c" when it is followed by "a," "o," or "u," and with a "k" when it is followed by "e" or "i." What happens if we *do* put "c" before "e" or "i"? It has an "s" sound!

/s/ = ce

cent	cell	cel-e-brate
cer-ti-fy	cen-ter	cel-er-y
cease	celebrate	ce-ment

Whenever a word ends with "-ce," the "e" is silent. Read down:

ace	prince	ice	twice
pace	prance	rice	spice
lace	Grace	lice	price
face	trace	nice	slice
mace	brace	mice	mince
face	space	dance	since
fleece	place	dunce	choice

You may find the WORST ENEMY or BEST FRIEND within YOURSELF!

mince ice	nice face	since race
place cent	spice rice	center lace
pace twice	trace Grace	price celery
cement cell	certify dunce	Grace dance
cease dance	prince prance	ace celebrate

"ci" usually has a short "i" sound, but it *can* have a long "i" sound as well:

/s/ = ci, cy

civ-il	cin-der	cin-e-ma	ci-der (long "i")
cir-cus	cir-cle	cit-y	cinema

The "y" in "cy" is usually pronounced /ī/:

cy-cle   cy-clone   cy-press

civil cinema	cycle cinema	cypress city
cyclone circle	cinder cider	circle circus

This brings us to *another* long-vowel digraph. When the /ē/ digraph "ie" has a "c" in front of it, the spelling usually changes. It becomes "ei." Knowing this rule will *really help* your spelling!

There is an easy way to remember this:
"I" BEFORE "E" EXCEPT AFTER "C."

/ē/ = ei

re-ceive	re-ceipt (The "p" is silent.)	ceil-ing
con-ceive	de-ceive	con-ceit

receive ceiling	conceive deceit
conceiving deceit	receiving conceit
received receipt	deceiving ceiling

To BREAK a bad habit ...   ... **DROP IT!**

Grace receive	Grace will receive a price of ten cents for that nice lace.
horse prances	The black horse prances and dances in his center cell.
races receive	Gus races to receive his cider, rice, celery, and mince pie.
cycle cinema	Let us cycle to the cinema and see a circus film twice!
cyclone ceiling	Since the cyclone hit, it left a center space in the ceiling.
prince circled	The prince circled the dance twice to be with Grace.
cypress circle	Big, old cypress trees circle that nice place in the city.
cel-e-brate spiced	Shall we celebrate with spiced cider at a fancy dance?

BAD   HABIT

Vowel Diphthongs

So far we have learned about digraphs—two letters that make one sound. Now we shall learn about DIPHTHONGS. A diphthong is two vowels that make *two* sounds, which blend and slide together continu-ously and are treated as one, in the same syllable. There are two spell-ing patterns for the /oi/ diph-thong: "oi" and "oy." The diacritical mark for /oi/ is "oi." Read down each column:

coins

/oi/ = oi

(/oi/ is usually spelled "oi" when it is in the middle of a word.)

oil	void	moist	coin
boil	avoid	hoist	loin
toil	noise	foist	join
foil	noisy	poise	joint
soil	broil	voice	point
coil	spoil	choice	oint-ment
poi-son	tin-foil	re-joice	ap-point-ment

Remember to read the longer words by syllables, covering up part of the word first if you need to (see page 58).
Or, simply put your finger under each syllable as you read it!

(Lessons are a little bit harder now, aren't they? Think of this: EVERYTHING is difficult before it is EASY!)

moist soil	boil oil	noise spoil
boil ointment	avoid poison	join tabloid
choice coin	voice rejoice	point coil
appointment	broil tinfoil	noisy voice
rejoice toil	spoil loin	point choice

oy = /oi/

(Sometimes this sound is spelled "oy" in the middle of a word, but it is *always* spelled "-oy" at the *end* of a word.)

boy	soy	en-joy	Roy
Joyce	de-stroy	con-voy	an-noy
toy	oys-ter	joy-ful	em-ploy

enjoy soy	joyful Roy	boy enjoys
toy oyster	annoy Joyce	employ Joy
boys annoy	destroy convoy	enjoy oyster

OI = OI, OY REVIEW

moist tinfoil	The boy broils his moist fish in tinfoil and enjoys it.
Joyce joining	Joyce enjoys joining Roy to play with his toy coins.
noisy annoys	The boy's noisy voice annoys Joyce and spoils her nap.
spoiled oyster	Roy's spoiled, green oyster is poison. Avoid it!
enjoy boiled	Gus and Joy enjoy boiled eggs in soy oil.

Never FLY into a RAGE unless you are prepared for a ROUGH LANDING ...

/ou/ = ou

mouse

There are also two spelling patterns for the /ou/ sound: "ou" and "ow." The diacritical mark for this sound is "ou." (/ou/ is usually spelled "ou" at the beginning or in the middle of a word.) Read down each column:

out	ouch	bound	house
scout	couch	a-bound	mouse
trout	pouch	pound	douse
shout	crouch	sound	blouse
spout	grouch	found	our
loud	proud	mound	sour
cloud	hound	round	flour
slouch	mount	a-round	foul
mouth	count	ground	bout
boun-ty	ac-count	as-tound	a-bout

> *Failure is not defeat unless you STOP TRYING ...*
> *Kites rise AGAINST the wind, not WITH it!*

Read across:

shout ouch	our hound	loud sound
round ground	sour flour	scout about
hound crouch	lout slouch	found pouch
proud mount	douse trout	cloud wound
mouth sound	mouse house	around mound

/ou/ = ow

(This sound is always spelled "-ow" when it occurs at the end of a word. It is also found in the middle of words that have multiple syllables, or end in "l" or "n.")

Read down each column:

how	town	tow-er	owl
cow	gown	pow-er	fowl
now	down	cow-er	howl
vow	frown	flow-er	jowl
wow	crown	show-er	growl
pow	drown	glow-er	yowl
bow	brown	chow-der	scowl
vow-el	clown	pow-der	prowl
tow-el	crowd	browse	how-dy

If you don't learn to laugh at trouble NOW, you won't have ANYTHING to laugh at when you grow OLD!

owl frown	bow down	down tower
prowl town	growl yowl	power vowel
how brown	fowl drown	flower power
brown gown	cower down	howdy crowd
clown howl	brown crown	shower towel
yowl scowl	crowd browse	cow chowder

Vowel Diphthong Review

found tower	proud scout	town house
mouse growl	joyful choice	found towel
brown trout	moist oyster	round flower
avoid boy	noisy crowd	hound howl
frown ouch	shout howdy	annoy Joyce

oysters boiled   Gus found moist oysters and boiled them in brown oil.

ointment joint   Rub ointment on the cow's sore joint to avoid a boil.

joyful hound   The joyful hound found a toy mouse in Roy's house.

count brown   Did you count the brown, round trout in our lake?

proud scouts   How proud our Roy is now at joining Boy Scouts!

frown-ing
growl-ing   Avoid that noisy, shouting, frowning, growling crowd!

Many a man's TONGUE broke his NOSE!

/j/ = ge, gi, gy

The /j/ sound at the end of a word usually is spelled "-ge." It is spelled "gi," "ge," or "gy" in the beginning or middle of a word.

age	rage	cage	page
sage	wage	stage	huge
range	hinge	lunge	large
change	germ	plunge	giant
gin-ger	gen-er-al	gy-rate	gentle
frig-id	dan-ger	o-rig-i-nal	Marge

lunge cage	fringe stage	huge wage
Marge rage	hinge barge	large range
danger change	plunge stage	original page

change original	Please change the old, original hinge on Marge's range.
plunge danger	The huge cats plunge and gyrate in rage. They smell danger!
Marge wage	Marge, please change my wage, and make it large.
lunge frigid	They lunge in rage in the huge cage on the frigid barge.

The only GOOD LUCK that many great people had was the determination to overcome BAD LUCK!

/j/ = -dge

To make the /j/ sound at the end of some *short-vowel* words we must add a "d" before the "-ge." We need a double consonant in order to keep the short-vowel sound.

edge	fudge	Madge	lodge
hedge	pudg-y	badge	dodge
ledge	budge	badg-er	sludge
wedge	judge	ridge	trudge
pledge	nudge	ledg-er	smudge

---

edge ledge	Madge budge	judge lodge
pledge badge	smudge fudge	dodge ledge
hodge-podge	pudgy Madge	hedge wedge

---

edge ledge	They trudge to the edge of the ledge on the ridge.
Madge dodges	Madge dodges the huge badger by the edge of the hedge.
pudgy fudge	Pudgy Gus gobbles huge wedges of ginger fudge in the lodge.
hodge-podge	His room is a hodgepodge of sludge. He pledges to clean it.

A winner LISTENS ... a loser just waits until it is HIS turn to TALK!

/j/ = ge, gi, gy, -dge Review

Madge charge — Madge and Marge charge up the edge of the ridge.

plunges large — Madge plunges off the large bridge near the lodge.

trudges lodge — Pudgy Gus trudges to the lodge for a huge plate of fudge.

badger gyrates — The badger gyrates and wedges himself under the stage.

Marge pledges — Marge pledges that she will not judge the change in Madge.

dodges ridge — Sage dodges the ridge and edges away from the barge.

huge smudge — There is a huge smudge of fudge on the edge of Gus' page.

danger edge — The large badgers smell danger by the edge of the hedge.

Make your life a LIGHT TO OTHERS ...
A candle loses nothing of its light
by lighting another candle.
Brighten the corner where YOU are!

Fluency Reality Check
-ge, gi-, & -dge Nonsense Words

Here is another list of nonsense words with "-ge" and "-dge" endings to check your knowledge of this phonics rule. Have your students read about six of these words out loud, and then choose six "real" words from the left-hand column on the previous page. Each group of words should be read with approximately the same ease, speed, and accuracy. (Remember: to keep the short-vowel sound there must be two consonants after the vowel. Otherwise, it's a long-vowel sound.)

Here are some short-vowel nonsense words:

senge	modge	runge	lenge	wirge
bidge	dudge	ginge	frunge	kirge

Here are a few long-vowel nonsense words:

vuge	bage	lige	stege	pluge
hege	slage	pruge	chige	wege

… And *here* are short- *and* long-vowel nonsense words mixed together!

rudge	ruge	penge	pege	frunge
fruge	linge	lige	credge	moge
bidge	nige	denge	dage	dradge
gide	modge	kange	pedge	nege
duge	dudge	fedge	fage	menge
slange	crige	crudge	suge	brenge

-y, -ie Plus Suffixes

When we add a suffix beginning with a vowel (such as -es, -ed, -er, or -est) to a word ending in "-y," we must first change the "y" to "i," and then add the suffix. Exception: we *keep* the "y" before adding "-ing." Read across:

try	tries	tried	try-ing
dry	dries	dried	dry-ing
spy	spies	spied	spy-ing
cry	cries	cried	cry-ing
re-ply	re-plies	re-plied	re-ply-ing
de-ny	de-nies	de-nied	de-ny-ing
stud-y	stud-ies	stud-ied	stud-y-ing
car-ry	car-ries	car-ried	car-ry-ing

silly	silli-er	silli-est
funny	funni-er	funni-est
misty	misti-er	misti-est
bumpy	bumpi-er	bumpi-est
early	earli-er	earli-est

When a word ENDS with "-ie," we drop the final "e," and then add the suffix. Exception: we change the "ie" to "y" before adding "-ing."

lie	lies	lied	ly-ing
tie	ties	tied	ty-ing
die	dies	died	dy-ing

-f = -ves

To make words ending in "-f" plural, we must first change the "f" to a "v," and then add "-es." Read across the page:

loaf	loaves	wife	wives
leaf	leaves	elf	elves
life	lives	shelf	shelves
thief	thieves	wolf	wolves
be-lief	be-lieves	re-lief	re-lieves

-Y, -IE PLUS SUFFIXES, AND -F = -VES REVIEW

funny crying	funniest cry
drying babies	dried baby
earliest leaf	early leaves
wife crying	wives cried
wolf carries	wolves carry
reply believing	replying belief
denied reply	denying replies
trying study	tried studying
elf believes	elves believed
wolf dying	wolves died
loaf drying	loaves dried
thief lying	thieves lied

FEAR *is the darkroom where* NEGATIVES *are developed ...*

-y, -ie Plus Suffixes, and –f = ves Review

wolves carried	The huge wolves carried the five crying cubs down the hill.
wives believe	The wives believe that the tiniest babies are lying asleep.
replied loaves	He replied, "Gus denied eating ten loaves of fried cake."
tried spying	Gus tried spying on elves flying in the earliest, mistiest leaves.
cried studying	They cried and tried studying for the earliest test.
believe funnier	I tried to believe that the old joke can get funnier and funnier.
tried replying	He tried replying that his shelves seemed the bumpiest.

It's NOT how hard you FALL ... it's how **HIGH** *you* **BOUNCE!**

New Vowel Sounds

So far, we have learned some vowel sounds, such as /o͞o/ in "food," page 169). There is *another* sound Read across the page. (Consider ties that begin on page 255 to rein-

book

digraphs that have *long-vowel* which has a long "u" sound (see that "oo" makes: /o͝o/ as in "book." using some of the games and activi-force the lessons. They're *fun!*)

/o͝o/ = oo

look	cook	cook-ie	cook-ies
good	wood-en	hood	stood
book	brook	took	nook
shook	soot	wool	hook
woof	roof	foot	foot-step

sooty cookie	good book	took hood
stood brook	wood foot	woof woof
wool hook	footstep	shook hoof
crooked book	hook foot	look cookies

look sooty — Look at that sooty, wooden roof!

stood brook — We stood in the brook and shook.

good cookies — Look, Gus took ten good cookies!

cookbooks — Good cooks look at good cookie cookbooks.

Courage

We CAN'T LEARN how to be BRAVE if we've only had WONDERFUL THINGS happen to us!

/ŏŏ/ = **oul**

"oul" is not really a digraph, but it has the same sound as the digraph we have just learned, /ŏŏ/. There are only a few words with this combination:

> could   would   should

/ŏŏ/ = **u**

There is a small group of words in which "u" has this sound as well. When reading books later, if you are not sure what sound the "u" makes in a word, try reading it with both /ŭ/ and /ŏŏ/. You will soon see which sound fits! Read across the page:

pull	full	bull	bul-let
push	push-y	bush	bush-y
put	put-ting	pud-ding	pul-ling

/ŏŏ/ = OO, OUL, U REVIEW

could put	should push	full bush
bushy hoof	would pull	put pudding
would push	bull could	bullet could
full bush	pushy bull	pulling bull
could push	should put	full pudding
would look	brook could	should cook
bullet shook	foot would	roof should

If you AIM HIGH, you can't SHOOT yourself in the FOOT!

/ŏŏ/ = oo, oul, u Review

would cook	He would cook if he could just find a good cookbook.
stood putting	I stood and shook, putting one foot in the brook near the woods.
should look	I should look at that good book. Would you put it down?
took pudding	Gus took a good cookbook and cooked a pot full of pudding.
could push	We could put a hook on the hood, and push and pull it.
stood wooden	The good pup stood in the bushes on a wooden box. Woof!
pushed sooty	He pushed the sooty bull's hoof. It stood and looked mad.
look wool	Look, this wool is full of hooks!

SAY what you MEAN,
and MEAN what you SAY ...
but **DON'T** say it **MEAN!**

/ô/ = au, aw, al, all, o

The diacritical mark for this sound is called a circumflex. Try looking up one of these words in the dictionary. "Haul," for example, is shown as "hôl." Read down each group of words:

/ô/ = au

Paul	pause		sauce	Maude
haul	cause	ball	fault	clause

Paul pause	haul sauce	cause Maude
Maude fault	pause clause	Paul sauce

/ô/ = aw

(This sound is spelled "aw" when it occurs at the *end* of a word.)

saw	jaw	dawn	thaw
law	paw	yawn	crawl
hawk	draw	lawn	shawl

> *People who just WAIT for something to TURN UP might BEGIN with their OWN SHIRTSLEEVES!*

/ô/ = AU, AW REVIEW

draw jaw	paw claw	Paul's jaw
cause law	saw dawn	draw claw
haul lawn	crawl lawn	hawk pause
thaw sauce	Maude yawn	fault clause
hawk crawl	Maude's shawl	pause dawn

/ô/ = al

When the letter "a" is followed by "l" it usually sounds like /ô/. Read across:

halt	hal-ter	false	fal-ter
al-so	al-most	al-ways	salt
al-ter	al-ter-nate	bald	scald

alter salt	almost bald	also scald
also halt	almost halt	always halt
always falter	false halter	also alternate

/ô/ = all

(This sound is spelled "-all" at the *end* of a word.)

all	wall	mall	fall
tall	stall	call	call-ing
hall	ball	small	small-er

/Ô/ = AL, ALL REVIEW

tall hall	all bald	alter ball
also fall	small wall	false salt
scald ball	falter stall	also small
almost tall	always halt	small halter

*It's nice to know
that when you
HELP someone up a HILL
you're a little nearer to the top YOURSELF!*

/Ô/ = O

"o" is not a digraph, but in a number of words the "o" has the "ô" sound instead of "ŏ." The sounds are very similar, but the name of something to eat will quickly show you the difference:

hŏt dôg

When reading books, if you are not sure which sound the word has, try both. *One* will fit! Read across the page:

dog	hog	fog	log
clog	smog	frog	lost
boss	cost	off	of-fer
soft	loft	floss	cross
moss	loss	toss	frost

/Ô/ = AU, AW, AL, ALL, O REVIEW

salt hog	dog paw	Paul tall
crawl fog	hog sauce	call dog
tall hawk	lawn cost	call boss
also offer	cross lawn	all sauce
frog yawn	frost thaw	crawl loft
dog halter	false dawn	lost shawl
toss floss	almost clog	saw smog
soft dawn	Maude cross	moss lawn
small frog	always yawn	small fault

Hardening of the HEART ages people more quickly than hardening of the ARTERIES ...

/ô/ = au, aw, al, all, o Review

Please, PLEASE continue to TAKE YOUR TIME with each lesson. You are reading VERY WELL by now, but these lessons are more complicated and take more time to read with ease. Remember this: professional football players or dancers are not good just because they already KNOW the game or the dance. They perform so well because they spend a LOT OF TIME practicing the things they ALREADY KNOW!

small yawns	His small pup yawns and crawls on his paws to the ball.
hawk almost	We saw the small hawk almost fall on the frosty lawn.
cross offered	Gus felt cross when he saw all the roast hog offered for dinner.
all halted	They all halted and saw the soft, pink dawn cross the sky.
frog draw	I saw a small frog I could almost draw, and also a dog.
always halts	Paul always halts and crawls on the tall, mossy log in the fog.
Maude soft	Maude offers almost all her cash for the small, soft dog.
Paul floss	Paul did not always floss, and he lost almost all his teeth.

Three-Consonant Beginnings

So far we have had words with double-consonant beginnings, as in "trip." Now let's read words with *three-letter* consonant beginnings. Read down each group:

rip	ray	ream	ice
trip	pray	cream	rice
strip	spray	scream	thrice
rain	rap	lat-ter	ash
train	trap	plat-ter	rash
strain	strap	splat-ter	thrash
ripe	ray	ram	roll
tripe	tray	cram	troll
stripe	stray	scram	stroll

The *first* word is also part of the *second* word in each phrase below. (Note, however, that they have different meanings.) Read across the page:

at splat	rap scrap	lit split
ill thrill	raw straw	rub scrub
lint splint	lash splash	rice thrice
ape scrape	row throw	retch stretch
ink sprinkle	ring string	lend splendid
ream stream	rush thrush	ram scramble

*We make a LIVING by what we GET ...
but we make a LIFE by what we GIVE!*

Practice a group of these words at a time, reading down. Then read them *across*. (It's fun to use these words with one of the activities or games beginning on page 255!)

thr-	**str-**	**scr-**	**spl-**
thrill	strip	scrap	split
threw	straw	scratch	splat
three	street	scream	splash
throat	string	scrub	splint
thrash	strap	scrape	splin-ter
thrush	stream	screen	splat-ter
thrown	strong	scruff	sprin-kle
throw	stroke	scram-ble	splen-did
thrice	stretch	scruf-fy	splay
thread	strange	Scrooge	splut-ter

All of these words contain *short vowels*. Read down, then across:

strap	scrap	thrash	splat
strip	scrub	throb	split
struck	scratch	thrill	splen-did

All of these words contain *long vowels*. Read down, then across:

stray	scrape	three	thrice
street	screen	throw	spray
strike	scream	three	stroke

The words in each phrase begin with the *same* three-letter consonant blend:

three thrush	strip string	straw strap
throat thrill	threw three	split spleen
split splinter	stroll street	spring sprint
throw thrash	strain strap	scrimp scrap
strong stroke	stripe strife	stream stretch
splatter splint	scrub scrape	splendid splash
scratch scream	scruffy screen	scramble scream

The words in these phrases begin with *different* three-letter blends:

scrub strip	throw splat	three strikes
straw splinter	spray street	thrash Scrooge
stroke throat	three splints	stretch thread
thrush splash	threw screen	splendid street
splatter stream	splendid stroll	scratchy throat
sprinkle splatter	strong splinter	scruffy spread
strip sprinkler	strain scramble	spring thrush
strange script	throw strike	thrifty scrap

The GREATEST IGNORANCE is to reject something you know NOTHING ABOUT!

Phonics Pathways: Clear Steps to Easy Reading and Perfect Spelling   **197**

Three-Consonant Beginnings Review

Read as many of these sentences as you can. It may take several efforts to read them all—just read what you can, and save the rest for another day.

(And remember: try to incorporate some of the activities and games beginning on page 256 when doing these lessons. These words can be difficult to read, and making a game out of it helps take the pressure off and makes it more fun as well!)

splashes splatters — The rain splashes and splatters as it strikes the strong screen.

scrapes splendid — Gus scrapes and scrubs the splendid cream on his plate.

three strange — Three strange flies thrash and strain in the strong bug strip.

stream splashes — The stream splashes and sprays my three backpack straps.

splendid thrush — We scramble and strain to stroke the splendid spring thrush.

thrashed strikes — The boy screamed and thrashed as he threw three strikes!

scratched scraped — She scratched and scraped her splinter, and it throbbed.

scrambles strains — Gus scrambles and strains as he strolls up the scruffy street.

Life is more FUN when you DON'T KEEP SCORE!

Short-Vowel Spelling Patterns

/ĕ/ = ea

On page 99 we learned that the digraph "ea" sounds like /ē/. Sometimes it sounds like /ĕ/ as well. Read across the page:

dead	read	bread
breath	deaf	head
heav-y	stead-y	read-y
weath-er	leath-er	feath-er
heav-en	leav-en	sweat-er
wealth	health	in-stead

/ĕ/ = a, ai

In a few words, /ĕ/ is spelled "a" or even "ai"! Read down the page:

any	a-gain	foun-tain
many	said	moun-tain

OPTIMISM is that cheerful frame of mind
that enables a TEA KETTLE to SING
even though it's in HOT WATER up to its NOSE!

ready again	said deaf
breath said	health bread
wealth again	feather head
leather instead	heavy sweater
against mountain	steady fountain
heav-en-ly weather	any mountain

We have already learned that added to the end of a word. sounds like /ĭ/. Read across

/ĭ/ = y

"-y" sounds like /ē/ when it is In the *middle* of a word, "y" the page:

myth	gym	sym-bol
lyr-ic	crys-tal	cyn-ic
syr-up	typ-i-cal	sys-tem
Lynn	hymn (The "n" is silent.)	mys-ter-y
Flynn	hys-ter-ic-al	Syl-vi-a
syn-thet-ic	hyp-no-sis	sym-pa-thy

/ĭ/ = ui

In a few words "ui" can sound like /ĭ/ also. Read across the page:

build	built	builder
guild	guilt	guilty

guilty Lynn	typical builder
Flynn builds	Sylvia's guild
lyr-i-cal hymn	build-ing gym
crystal building	built cyl-in-der
synthetic syrup	sym-bol-ic myth
gym-nast guilty	hypnosis system
sym-pa-thet-ic Lynn	hys-ter-i-cal cynic

Even if you're on the RIGHT TRACK, you'll get RUN OVER if you just SIT there!

/ŏ/ = a

A few "a" words sound like /ŏ/.
Read across the page:

wand	wander	wasp
want	wanted	wanting
father	wanton	Wanda

Wanda wants   father wanders

/Ĕ/ = EA, AI; /Ĭ/ = Y, UI; AND /Ŏ/ = A REVIEW

Wanda read	deaf wasp
health system	Lynn wants
wants syrup	father builds
already guilty	Flynn read
heavy crystal	want leather
read mystery	crystal wand
steady fountain	wanton cynic
heav-en-ly hymn	symbol wealth
gymnast wanders	Cyril's sweater
mountain weather	typical builder
wants sym-pa-thy	Sylvia's feather
Wanda hys-ter-i-cal	wander mountain

More people RUST OUT than WEAR OUT ...

/ŭ/ = o

At times "o" is pronounced /ŭ/. These letters frequently have "m" or "n" next to them. Read across the page:

won	son	from	done
none	ton	mon-ey	some
lov-er	cov-er	a-bove	a-mong
shove	glove	com-fort	hon-ey
oth-er	moth-er	broth-er	a-noth-er
mon-key	don-key	noth-ing	Mon-day

one (wŭn)　　once (wŭns)　　of (ŭv)

/ŭ/ = ou

In a few words, "ou" sounds like /ŭ/:

touch	young	cous-in
couple	double	coun-try

Sometimes even "oo" and "a" sound like /ŭ/!

/ŭ/ = oo,　　/ŭ/ = a

flood blood　　　　was (wŭz)

was from	one glove	of another
love honey	once flood	above cover
of country	among some	once mother
from cousin	nothing done	donkey was
comfort son	touch monkey	ton of blood
double money	young couple	brother shove

Schwa /ŭ/ = ə

In multisyllable words, the unaccented vowel sounds (including vowel digraphs) often resemble /ŭ/. The diacritical mark for this sound is "ə." It is called a "schwa," a German word that means silence instead of a vowel sound. It isn't really silent, but is indefinite and neutral in sound. It certainly makes spelling a lot more complicated, since the schwa sound can represent *any one* of the vowels! You may prefer to just read these words for now, and learn to spell them later. (**Note:** The schwa sounds on this page are all highlighted.)

so´-fa	(a = ə)	so´-fŭ
spo´-ken	(e = ə)	spo´-kŭn
san´-i-ty	(i = ə)	san´-ŭ-ty
gal´-lop	(o = ə)	gal´-lŭp
fo´-cus	(u = ə)	fo´-cŭs

Many words beginning or ending with an unaccented "a" have the schwa sound:

a-rise´	a-woke´	a-lone´	a-way´
a-while´	a-void´	a-round´	a-cross´
at-tack´	at-tain´	at-tend´	at-tach´
tu´-ba	dra´-ma	ex´-tra	so´-fa
so´-da	chi´-na	ze´-bra	del´-ta
for´-mu-la	ba-nan´-a	um-brel´-la	va-nil´-la

We see it frequently with ending syllables, but the schwa can occur *anywhere*:

se´-cond	spi´-nal	dir-ect´	lem´-on
se´-rum	lov´-a-ble	les´-son	man´-age
cho´-sen	meth´-od	ve-loc´-i-ty	de-vel´-op

An APOLOGY is a GOOD WAY to have the LAST WORD ...

/ŭ/ = o, ou, oo, a, ə Review

glove another	Bud lost his glove but got another one from Mom.
double banana	Gus just loves to munch a double banana nut soda.
nothing done	Nothing was done to stop the flood from coming.
monkey shoved	One month a young monkey shoved my brother.
once blood	Once some blood was taken from my other son.
loved touch	Mother loved to touch the fat, young, fluffy puppy.

Problems can be OBSTACLES or STEPPING STONES, depending upon how we see them … (Obstacles are those depressing things we see whenever we stop looking at our GOALS.)

All of the vowels in the following sentence have the same sound: /ŭ/. Copy it, and circle all the different spelling patterns of this sound. Then write your *own* sentence, using as many of these spelling patterns as you can think of:

Once Bud's young pup was running from a flood.

Short-Vowel Spelling Patterns Review

The words in each phrase have the *same* short-vowel sound. Read across:

one ton	built gym
want father	double cover
won money	young couple
steady head	another flood
comfort son	country cousin

The words in each phrase have *different* short-vowel sounds. Read across:

once again	father ready
cover syrup	Lynn's cousin
build above	another hymn
steady couple	Monday again
touch crystal	wants mystery
typical father	wander mountain

father crystal	Lynn's father built another heavy crystal fountain in the country.
steady builds	Steady rain builds another flood in typical mountain weather.
again cover	Once again, it comforts Gus to cover banana nut bread with tons and tons and tons of honey syrup!

LEARN from the mistakes of OTHERS ...
for none of us can ever LIVE long enough to make them all OURSELVES!

Contractions

A CONTRACTION is what happens when *two words* are run together to make *one word*, and *one or more letters are removed* from the second word.

An APOSTROPHE is substituted for the missing letter(s). We use contractions as *shortcuts* when reading or speaking. Here is an example:

I am = Iam = I~~a~~m = I'm

is = 's

she is = she's
he is = he's
it is = it's

~~a~~re = 're

we are = we're
they are = they're
you are = you're

~~w~~ill = 'll

I will = I'll
he will = he'll
she will = she'll

we will = we'll
it will = it'll
you will = you'll

they will = they'll

n~~o~~t = n't

is not = isn't
are not = aren't
do not = don't
(dŭz) does not = doesn't
did not = didn't
can not = can't
could not = couldn't

was not = wasn't
were not = weren't
(hăv) have not = haven't
has not = hasn't
had not = hadn't
should not = shouldn't
would not = wouldn't

Contractions Review

Read and write each sentence. Then name the *original words* in each contraction:

It's raining.

You haven't eaten.

You're limping.

She'll eat later.

I wasn't kidding.

Isn't Gus funny?

I don't have it.

He can't swim yet.

Shouldn't we go?

He didn't sing well.

We're eating lunch.

He'll be careful.

They'll come soon.

They're running.

He's running very fast!

We aren't afraid.

They weren't asleep.

She doesn't think so.

I wouldn't trust him.

They couldn't sleep.

We'll move soon.

It'll be fine.

She's sick.

I'm going.

The windmill is moved BY its surroundings, but the electric fan MOVES its surroundings ... WHICH ONE ARE **YOU***?*

Silent Letters: -le

We have had a few silent letters so far, like the "magic e," the "e" in "-ce," and the "l" in "-ould." Here are some more. When a multisyllable word ends in unaccented "-le," the "e" is silent. On page 110 we learned that consonant endings on short-vowel words must be doubled before adding other endings. This is true for "-le" endings as well. Also, note how "-le" words are divided: except for "-ckle," the letter *before* the "-le" ending is kept *with* the "-le." Read down each group:

-ckle	-gle	-ble	-tle
tick-le	an-gle	gob-ble	tat-tle
pick-le	tan-gle	hob-ble	cat-tle
cack-le	bun-gle	bab-ble	lit-tle
crack-le	jun-gle	dab-ble	brit-tle
	jan-gle	bum-ble	ket-tle
	jin-gle	rum-ble	
-ple	tin-gle	tum-ble	**-zle**
sim-ple	sin-gle	crum-ble	siz-zle
sam-ple		grum-ble	fiz-zle
dim-ple		a-ble	raz-zle
pim-ple	**-dle**	ta-ble	daz-zle
top-ple	sad-dle	ca-ble	nuz-zle
ap-ple	pad-dle	fee-ble	puz-zle
	han-dle	bub-ble	ɑuz-zle
-fle	can-dle	dou-ble	
raf-fle	mid-dle	trou-ble	
ruf-fle	mud-dle	ter-ri-ble	
muf-fle	noo-dle	hor-ri-ble	
shuf-fle	poo-dle		

> *The LESS you talk, the MORE you are listened to!*

Silent -le Review

The words in each phrase mostly are the *same* except for the beginning letters:

razzle dazzle	tickle pickle	huddle cuddle
apple dapple	cattle tattle	simple dimple
feeble steeple	jingle jangle	middle riddle
sizzle fizzle	poodle noodle	double trouble
snuffle truffle	muddle puddle	mumble grumble

The words in these phrases are mostly *different,* and have different beginning letters:

shuffle table	gobble apple	humble Mable
kettle jingle	cattle hobble	little apple
double ruffle	tickle poodle	nibble truffle
puzzle tangle	jungle muddle	sample pickle
terrible trouble	horrible rumble	poodle puddle

tickle cuddle	Gus likes to tickle and cuddle his simple, little poodle.
middle muddle	I'm in the middle of a muddle as I fumble with this puzzle!
snuffles truffles	Gus snuffles truffles, and his poodle nibbles noodles.
kettle sizzles	The little kettle sizzles, fizzles, and bubbles on the table.

NOBODY ever left footprints in the sands of time by SITTING DOWN!

Phonics Pathways: Clear Steps to Easy Reading and Perfect Spelling **209**

Silent Letters: k, w, l, b, t, h

Silent letters can be complicated to learn. This section also may be more difficult because the vowel sounds are quite varied. Therefore, some of the more difficult words are written with diacritical marks for those of you who might find them helpful.

k

Read across the page:

knot	knob	knelt
knit	knit-ted	knit-ting
knock	knack	knuck-le
knife	know	known
knee	kneel	kneel-ing

w

wrist	wrap	wreck
wring	wrong	wrung
write	wreath	wrote

l

talk (tôk)	walk (wôk)	stalk (stôk)
half (hăf)	calf (kăf)	chalk (chôk)

knock wrist	knee kneel	stalk calf
wrong knee	knock chalk	write half
half wrong	wrote talk	calf kneel
wrap knife	knelt wreck	know walk
knitted wrap	know knack	wrong knob
wring knuckle	wrap wreath	known knot

b

dumb	numb	crumb
lamb	limb	bomb
climb	climb-ing	climb-er
comb	plumb-er	thumb-ing

People who are all wrapped up in themselves are OVERDRESSED!

t

of-ten (ôfən)	sof-ten (sôfən)	lis-ten (lĭsən)
nes-tle (nĕsəl)	wres-tle (rĕsəl)	wres-tling
lis-ten-ing	glis-ten (glĭsən)	cas-tle (kăsəl)
has-ten (hāsən)	chas-ten (chāsən)	whis-tle (wĭsəl)

h

hour (our)	hour-ly	ghet-to (gĕtō)
honest (ŏnəst)	hon-est-ly	honor (ŏnər)
ghost (gōst)	ghast-ly (găstlē)	ghoul (gool)

listen often	castle nestle	climb limb
lamb glisten	ghastly climb	listen ghetto
wrestle crumb	numb thumb	lamb nestle
often wrestle	dumb ghost	hourly climb
soften thumb	listen whistle	honest honor
plumber hasten	climbing limb	ghastly bomb

Phonics Pathways: Clear Steps to Easy Reading and Perfect Spelling **211**

Silent k, w, l, b, t, h Review

dumb lamb — The dumb lamb knows how to climb in my lap and nestle.

often talk — They often talk and whistle as they hasten up the peaks.

thumb knife — Gus cut his thumb with a knife when he ate half of the calf.

plumber knows — The plumber knows our sink well. Honestly, it is a wreck!

walk castle — We often walk to the castle and listen to the hourly talk.

kneels knocks — She kneels and knocks half of the knitting from her wrist.

knows knees — She knows how to walk on her knees and her thumbs.

honestly wrong — Honestly, this is the wrong walk. We must hasten home.

A mind stretched to a **NEW IDEA**
never goes back to its original dimensions!

Silent gh

There are three main patterns to silent "gh": "igh," "ough," and "augh." (Remember to put a piece of paper underneath the line you are reading if it makes it easier for you, or just move your finger underneath each word.) Read across the page:

/ī/ = igh

sigh	sight	plight
fight	flight	fright
tight	right	might
light	slight	bright
night	high	thigh

Each of us is born with TWO ENDS ...
one to SIT ON, and one to THINK WITH.
SUCCESS depends upon which
one we use more ...
HEADS *we* **WIN** ...
TAILS *we* **LOSE!**

light night	right flight	thigh high
might sigh	night fright	tight fight
right thigh	night light	slight sigh
might light	high flight	right sight
slight fight	bright light	sigh plight
fright sight	night flight	sight light

/ô/ = **ough, augh**

ought	fought	bought
thought	sought	brought
caught	taught	daugh-ter
slaugh-ter	haugh-ty	fraught
naugh-ty	naugh-ti-er	naugh-ti-est

/ō/ = **ough**

though	al-though
dough	thor-ough

/ou/ = **ough**

bough

Some people are a lot like BOATS ...
They TOOT LOUDEST when they're in a FOG!

crawl caught	Paul ought
fought cause	caught paw
brought salt	taught Paul
bought sauce	brought halter
halt slaughter	small daughter
sought dough	almost thought
although naughty	Maude thorough

Silent gh Review

might though — Gus might take a night flight, though he fights his fright.

brought right — Paul brought the right game. He thought it might be taught.

ought thought — She ought to have thought of her bright daughter.

small daughter — His small daughter might put bright lights on her high tree.

although caught — The thief fought, although he got caught in the night light.

sighed thought — I sighed as I thought of how I sought the right dog.

fight fright-ful — The fight was a frightful sight, and was brought to a halt. Maude was naughty!

 A smile is a CURVE that can set a lot of things STRAIGHT!

/ā/ Spelling Patterns

Sometimes "ei" and "eigh" sound like /ā/. Read across the page:

/ā/ = ei

vein	veil	skein
feign (silent "g")	rein	rein-deer

/ā/ = eigh

Here is a new verse to the poem we learned on page 170:

> *"I" before "e" except after "c,"*
> *or when sounding like /ā/*
> *as in "neighbor" and "weigh."*

eight	eighth	sleigh
weigh	weight	freight
neigh	neigh-ing	weigh-ing
neigh-bor	neigh-bor-ly	neigh-bor-hood

> *Keep yourself clean and bright ...*
> *YOU are the window through which*
> *you must see the WORLD!*

eight veils	neighbor	weigh veil
weigh freight	feign vein	weigh skein
vein weight	weigh sleigh	eight sleighs
reindeer neigh	eighth sleigh	neighborhood

There are two more spelling patterns for /ā/.
Read down the page:

/ā/ = ey

hey	prey	o-bey
they	grey	sur-vey

/ā/ = ea

steak	break	great
rump-steak	break-in	great-ness

The FRIENDS we choose are like ELEVATORS ...
They can help us RISE to the TOP,
or they can drag us DOWN to the BOTTOM!

/Ā/= EI, EIGH, EY, EA REVIEW

they feign	veil great	they prey
steak neigh	great veil	neighborly
sleigh rein	they obey	obey survey
they weigh	grey sleigh	weigh freight
great steak	sleigh straight	ate rump steak
eighth break	break survey	obey neighbor
weigh steak	rump steak	survey break-in

/ā/ Spelling Patterns Review

obeyed eighth	They obeyed and grabbed the eighth rein on the sleigh.
they survey	They survey their prey and think, "Great rumpsteak!"
neighborhood	They wore their great veils in the grey neighborhood.
eight gained	Gus ate eight great steaks, and he gained a lot of weight.
great break	They pray the great doctor will not break eight veins.
they sleigh	They played on a great sleigh pulled by eight tiny reindeer.
neighbors	Eight great neighbors stay to help weigh the freight.
eighteen	They had eighteen grey days of rain in Spain!

Don't just WAIT for opportunity to come knocking at your door ...
Go out and FIND it!
If you're looking for a BIG OPPORTUNITY, seek out a BIG PROBLEM ...
PROBLEMS are nothing but OPPORTUNITIES IN WORK CLOTHES!

s = /z/, /zh/, /sh/

On page 59 we learned four words in which "s" sounds like /z/: "is," "his," "as," and "has." Words ending in "-se" can also sound like /z/. Read across the page:

rose	pose	nose
rise	a-rise	wise
ease	tease	please
chose	choose	cheese
use	fuse	re-fuse
pause	clause	be-cause

Here are some words where "s" sounds like /zh/:　　a-zure

plea-sure　　　　mea-sure　　　　trea-sure

And here are two "s" words that sound like /sh/!

sure　　sugar

please pose	please rise	sugar nose
use treasure	measure nose	sure please
choose sugar	sure-ly please	tease Rose
azure treasure	measure fuse	wise because
chose pleasure	wise pleasure	refuse cheese

The real voyage of discovery consists not of seeking NEW LANDSCAPES, but of having NEW EYES!

pleased treasure	I am pleased beyond measure to win the azure treasure.
surely measure	It's surely not easy to measure the alligator's long nose.
pleasure because	Gus gets pleasure because his nose is in sugar and cheese.
pauses refuses	Rose pauses and wisely refuses to choose the easy path.
chose because	She chose to pause because the azure rose was thorny.
arises pauses	He arises, pauses, and blows his nose. He surely has a cold!
refuses teasing	He refuses to stop teasing Gus. Rose pauses, rises, and says: "Please do not tease Gus *any more!*"

*Happiness is not the ABSENCE of conflict, but the ability to COPE with it …
It takes both sunshine AND rain to make a LOVELY RAINBOW!*

/f/ = ph

Read across the page:

phone   pho-ny   tel-e-phone
phys-ics   phys-i-cal   Phil-ip
pam-phlet   el-e-phant   phan-tom
phon-ics   or-phan   pho-to-graph
phase   phrase   pho-no-graph

phony phantom   elephant photo
telephone orphan   orphan elephant
physics pamphlet   physical phase
phantom photograph   phonics phrase
Philip's phonograph   Phil's telephone

/f/ = gh

rough (rŭf)   e-nough (enŭf)   tough (tŭf)
laugh (lăf)   laugh-ing   cough (kôf)

FREEDOM begins between your EARS!

tough	cough	laugh	enough
rough	laugh	enough	coughing
enough	laughing	tough	enough

/f/ = ph, gh Review

Read across:

tough physical	tough phrase
elephant cough	rough cough
telephone Phil	phony telephone
Philip laugh	Philip photograph
enough phonics	enough laughter
laughing orphan	laughing elephant

laugh phantom — They laugh and laugh at the phony phantom.

telephone rough — Telephone Phil. He has a rough cough and is in bed.

elephant tough — Be careful! That elephant is tough and rough.

orphan enough — That orphan has had enough rough times. Let's help!

photograph Phil — Photograph Phil and his fancy physics pamphlet.

Phil phonics — Both Phil and Gus have had enough phonics for today.

TRYING TIMES are NOT the times to STOP TRYING!

/k/ = ch

Sometimes "ch" can sound like /k/! Read across the page:

chord	chor-us	ache
chron-ic	chron-i-cle	chem-ist
school	schol-ar	schol-as-tic
Chris-tie	chris-ten	Christ-mas (The "t" is silent.)
scheme	sched-ule	Chris-to-pher

---

christen Chris	school chronicle
chronic chord	chemist scheme
Christmas chorus	Christie scholar
Christopher ache	scholastic schedule

---

schedule Christie — Shall we schedule a day to christen baby Christie?

chemist scheme — The chemist has a scheme that cures a chronic cough.

Christopher aches — Christopher aches to sing in the Christmas chorus.

school schedule — Chris has a very long school schedule this year.

ATTITUDE is the mind's PAINTBRUSH ...
It can COLOR any situation!

Another r-Modified Vowel Sound

When "e" is added to a word *ending* in "-ar," it makes an *entirely new* r-modified vowel sound, which sounds like "air." There are several ways to spell this sound. Read across the page:

bear

/âr/ = -are

fare	care	bare	dare
share	stare	glare	rare
spare	scare	snare	mare
ware	blare	flare	pare

/âr/ = -air

air	fair	pair	hair
lair	stair	flair	chair

/âr/ = -ear

bear	tear	wear	pear

/âr/ = -ere

there (refers to "direction")   where

ONE MORE word has this sound. It sounds exactly like "there," but is spelled differently and has a completely different meaning:

their (means "belonging to them")

Where are their cakes? Over there?

/âr/ = -are, -air, -ear, -ere, -eir Review

dare bear	fare there	their pair
flair wear	rare pear	snare lair
bare chair	bear stare	stair there
scare bear	share flare	fair Claire
their mare	Mary cares	where hare

share chair Mary, please share that fair chair over there with Claire.

where hairy Where is their rare pair of black hairy bears?

stare tear They dare to stare at the tear in my spare pair of pants.

scary bears The scary bears glare and stare in their lair under the stairs.

Blair pears Mary and Blair stare at their fair share of rare pears.

dares wear Mary dares Gus to wear his pair of rare boots to the fair.

The GREATEST OAK was once a LITTLE NUT that HELD ITS GROUND!

A Spelling Grab Bag

This section deals with some spelling rules that are really useful to know. Just look them over for now. You can learn them more thoroughly at a later date:

Homonyms

Strictly speaking, true *homonyms* have the *same* sound and spelling, but *different meanings*. The meaning needed is determined by the context of the word within the sentence:

I can read well. We can apples in the fall.
I cannot bear snakes. He saw big bear tracks.
That rose is very red. I rose from my chair.

Homophones

On pages 169 and 170 we learned about words that *sound* the same, as homonyms do, but have different *spellings* as well as meanings, such as "too," "to," and "two." (See also "their" and "there" on page 224.) These words are called *homophones*.

Homophones certainly make life complicated when it comes to spelling! The more you read, however, the better you will be able to select the correct spelling when you need to write any of these words.

Write a simple sentence using each of the words listed below. Use the dictionary to find out the meaning of any word you are unsure of:

here hear	to two too
do due	blue blew
shoo shoe	pane pain
break brake	steak stake
no know	great grate
shone shown	there their
raise rays	steel steal
cheep cheap	choose chews

If you can't get people to listen any other way, tell them it's a **SECRET!**

(SSshhhhhhhh)

There are many more. I'll bet *you* can think of some that are not listed here! It's fun to keep a list and see how many you can come up with.

Homographs

Homographs, like homonyms, are words that are spelled the same way and have different meanings. But homographs usually have different *pronunciations* also! As with homonyms, it's easy to determine which meaning we need, just by reading the sentence. This "context clue" will tell us exactly which word fits.

Ben likes to read books.

Ben read a book today.

> *Learn from the OYSTER ... with a LITTLE GRIT it can produce a PEARL!*

The actor took a bow at the end of the play.

Katie had a big, fat, pink bow in her hair.

We live in a small, wooden house.

I like to hear a live band best of all!

Gus got a big tear in his best pants.

Jan felt sad, and a tear rolled down her cheek.

The dove sang and sang in the big pine tree.

Jan dove in the water, but bumped her head.

Gus will lead us to the table with cream cakes.

Gus' tummy feels as heavy as a lump of lead.

Homonym, Homophone, & Homograph Chart

	SOUND	SPELLING	MEANING
HOMONYMS	Same	Same	Different
HOMOPHONES	Same	Different	Different
HOMOGRAPHS	Different	Same	Different

Multisyllable Words with Suffixes

On page 70 we learned that when we add a suffix beginning with a vowel to a single-syllable, short-vowel word ending with only *one* consonant, we *double* that consonant before adding the suffix. In a *multisyllable,* short-vowel word, if the accent is on the *last syllable,* we *also* double the last consonant before adding these suffixes, in order to keep the short-vowel sound. Read across the page

sub-mit´	sub-mit´-ted	sub-mit´-ting
ad-mit	ad-mit-ted	ad-mit-ting
per-mit	per-mit-ted	per-mit-ting
com-pel	com-pel-led	com-pel-ling

If the accent is *not* on the last syllable, we *do not* double the final consonant before adding these suffixes:

mar´-ket	mar´-ket-ed	mar´-ket-ing
vis-it	vis-it-ed	vis-it-ing
trum-pet	trum-pet-ed	trum-pet-ing
hap-pen	hap-pen-ed	hap-pen-ing

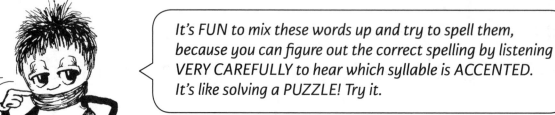

It's FUN to mix these words up and try to spell them, because you can figure out the correct spelling by listening VERY CAREFULLY to hear which syllable is ACCENTED. It's like solving a PUZZLE! Try it.

admitted	visited	permitted
submitting	trumpeting	visiting
happened	compelled	marketed
permitting	happening	admitting
submitted	trumpeted	submitting
compelling	marketing	permitting

-ce, -ge

When a word ends in "-ce" or "-ge," we keep the "e" before adding "-ous" or "-able." This keeps the "j" sound of "g" and the "s" sound of "c":

out-ra-geous	gor-geous	cou-ra-geous
peace-able	change-able	trace-able
no-tice-able	re-place-able	dam-age-able

-able, -ible

If a word is complete in itself *without* the ending, we usually spell it "-able." If not, most of the time (but not always!) we spell it "-ible":

read-able	tax-able	crush-able
suit-able	pack-able	pre-fer-able
bend-able	mend-able	pre-vent-able
cred-ible	vis-ible	ed-ible
pos-sible	ter-rible	com-pat-ible

*People are like stained glass windows ...
They SPARKLE and SHINE
when the sun is out,
but when the darkness sets in
their TRUE BEAUTY is revealed
ONLY if there is LIGHT WITHIN!*

Prefixes

A PREFIX is a syllable that is attached to the front of a word. Usually this changes the word's meaning. There are many prefixes, but we shall try just a few:

pre-   (means "before," or "in front of")

pre-mix	pre-cool	pre-heat
pre-judge	pre-ma-ture	pre-pay

sub-   (means "under," or "beneath")

sub-way	sub-let	sub-ma-rine
sub-di-vide	sub-mit	sub-tract
sub-con-tract	sub-arc-tic	sub-merge

re-   (usually means "again," or "back")

re-act	re-do	re-copy
re-cov-er	re-place	re-paint
re-heat	re-fresh	re-turn

auto-   (means "by oneself," or "by itself")

auto-mat	auto-mo-bile	auto-bus
auto-mat-ic	auto-mo-tive	auto-graph

> A DWARF standing on the shoulders
> of a GIANT
> can see FARTHER
> than the
> GIANT HIMSELF!

un- (means "the reverse of")

un-zip	un-like	un-kind
un-able	un-seen	un-cov-er
un-done	un-hap-py	un-luck-y

dis- (means "the reverse of")

dis-able	dis-a-gree	dis-col-or
dis-pose	dis-o-bey	dis-cov-er

inter- (means "between two things")

inter-act	inter-com	inter-lock
inter-mix	inter-change	inter-view

super- (means "extra," or "above")

super-mom	super-heat
super-son-ic	super-vise
super-vi-sor	super-no-va
super-hu-man	super-pow-er
super-sen-si-tive	super-mar-ket
super-in-ten-dent	super-im-pose

The DIFFICULTIES in life are meant to make us BETTER, not BITTER!

Prefix Review

re-dis-cov-er super-no-va
rediscover supernova

inter-view super-mom
interview supermom

un-hap-py super-vi-sor
unhappy supervisor

inter-view super-pow-er
interview superpower

sub-merge sub-ma-rine
submerge submarine

pre-judge super-in-ten-dent
prejudge superintendent

sub-arc-tic super-mar-ket
subarctic supermarket

super-sen-si-tive auto-mo-bile
supersensitive automobile

The best and most beautiful things in the world cannot be SEEN or TOUCHED but are FELT in the HEART!

More Suffixes

You have been introduced to suffixes in previous lessons—here are some more. (The "-tion" or "-sion" suffix is pronounced "/shun/.")

/shun/ = -tion

sta-tion	ac-tion	
na-tion	ad-di-tion	
por-tion	ad-dic-tion	
sec-tion	at-ten-tion	
va-ca-tion	af-fec-tion	
pro-mo-tion	in-vi-ta-tion	
ed-u-ca-tion	foun-da-tion	

/shun/ = -sion

vi-sion
mis-sion
ex-ten-sion
ex-plo-sion
ex-pres-sion
im-pres-sion
tel-e-vi-sion

-able

dur-able	en-able	dis-able
de-sir-able	ca-pable	no-table
a-dor-able	val-u-able	port-able
rea-son-able	pass-able	print-able
for-mi-dable	in-ca-pable	prob-able
pre-sent-able	per-ish-able	de-lec-table
pre-vent-able	im-prob-able	con-sid-er-able
in-es-cap-able	in-com-pa-rable	in-dis-pen-sable

When you were born, YOU cried and the WORLD rejoiced. Live your life in such a way that when you come to die, the WORLD cries, and YOU rejoice!

-ness

good-ness	thick-ness	ill-ness
kind-ness	weak-ness	dark-ness
mad-ness	soft-ness	well-ness
nice-ness	bad-ness	wil-der-ness

-ful (means "full of")

arm-ful	hope-ful	fear-ful
faith-ful	care-ful	pain-ful
play-ful	harm-ful	use-ful
won-der-ful	for-get-ful	thank-ful

-less (means "without")

rest-less	reck-less	need-less
shift-less	help-less	end-less
worth-less	price-less	time-less
hope-less	point-less	home-less

-ment

place-ment	move-ment	treat-ment
state-ment	base-ment	a-bate-ment
pun-ish-ment	re-place-ment	re-fresh-ment
pave-ment	en-gage-ment	gov-ern-ment

WHO is right is never so important as WHAT is right!

Suffix Review

won-der-ful in-vi-ta-tion
wonderful invitation

pre-sent-able gov-ern-ment
presentable government

in-com-pa-rable va-ca-tion
incomparable vacation

in-dis-pen-sable foun-da-tion
indispensable foundation

for-mi-dable mis-sion
formidable mission

de-sir-able pro-mo-tion
desirable promotion

a-dor-able ex-pres-sion
adorable expression

price-less wil-der-ness
priceless wilderness

The WORST PRISON of all is the one inside a CLOSED HEART.

Compound Words

A COMPOUND WORD is made by joining two complete words together to make a new word. It's fun to read the list below and determine which two words each one is made of! Compound words are *always* divided into the smaller words from which they are composed.

any-thing	hill-side	under-stand
classroom	without	bedroom
somebody	freeway	downtown
paycheck	clipboard	homework
sunrise	brainwash	earthquake
outdoors	supermarket	workout
datebook	overcome	pathways
superman	buckskin	footbridge
daybreak	hunchback	something
crackdown	tablecloth	underworld
playground	ballgame	homesick
	roommate	rosewood
	underground	footsteps

We can't stop the WAVES, but we can learn to SURF!

Building Blocks

In each group of words, the top word is a part of every word listed below it. You will be *building words* from *blocks of syllables.* Try it … it's *fun!*

board
board-ing
key-board
clip-board

check
check-er
re-check
pay-check

rage
en-rage
en-rag-ing
out-ra-geous

pass
under-pass
sur-pass-ing
un-sur-pass-able

back
back-ing
back-ward
out-back

front
front-ward
con-front
con-fron-ta-tion

press
ex-press
in-ex-press-ible
com-press-ing

cover
un-cover
un-re-cover-able
dis-cover-ing

May we have the grace
to ACCEPT the things we cannot change …
the courage to CHANGE the things we can …
and the WISDOM to know the DIFFERENCE!

mark
re-mark
re-mark-able
un-re-mark-able

come
wel-come
wel-com-ing
over-com-ing

see
fore-see
fore-see-able
un-fore-see-able

fort
com-fort
ef-fort
for-tress
ef-fort-less
com-fort-able
com-fort-ing-ly

sense
non-sense
sens-i-tive
super-sens-i-tive

force
en-force
force-ful-ness
re-in-force-ment

give
for-give
for-giv-able
un-for-giv-able

agree
agree-able
agree-ment
agree-ing
dis-agree
dis-agree-able
dis-agree-ment

WINNERS never QUIT ...
and QUITTERS never WIN!

tend	tract
in-tend	sub-tract
in-tend-ing	sub-tract-able
super-in-ten-dent	un-sub-tract-able
under	land
under-stand	land-mark
mis-under-stand	play-land
mis-under-stand-ing	out-land-ish
mark	pen
mar-ket	play-pen
mar-ket-ing	pen-cil
mar-ket-able	in-dis-pen-sa-ble
mar-ket-a-bil-i-ty	car-pen-ter
sent	press
pre-sent	im-press
pre-sent-ed	im-pres-sion
pre-sent-able	im-pres-sion-able
un-pre-sent-able	im-pres-sion-is-tic

FRIENDSHIP is like a BEAUTIFUL GARDEN ...
The more you put INTO it, the better it GROWS!

His won-der-ful, re-mark-able auto-mo-bile has a super-sen-si-tive inter-com.

A super-no-va is a fan-tas-tic star that can sud-den-ly shine a bil-lion times bright-er!

He seems to have a hope-less ad-dic-tion to worth-less tel-e-vi-sion pro-grams.

She went to con-sid-er-able length to be help-ful af-ter that dev-as-tat-ing earth-quake.

I have the im-pres-sion that Gus loves end-less por-tions of de-lec-table re-fresh-ments.

It is im-prob-able that we will dis-cov-er any more gold in that hill-side wil-der-ness.

Aus-tra-lia has out-land-ish-ly huge croc-o-diles in its re-mark-able out-back.

*Life itself can't give you joy,
    unless you really WILL it ...
Life just gives you
    time and space ...
It's up to YOU to FILL IT!*

Supermom's performance went fantastically well.

It is time to submerge the submarine. *NOW!*

I'm cold. This must be a subarctic supermarket.

Gus thinks he is going on a formidable mission.

Her cats possess the most adorable expressions.

Soon she is going on an incomparable vacation.

Phonics is an unsurpassable tool for reading.

His expression at that moment was unprintable.

A strong foundation is indispensable to a house.

… And now, my re-gret-ful but un-a-void-able and in-es-cap-able con-clu-sion is that we have just fin-ished this in-ten-sive and sub-stan-tial book. This is the end. GOODBYE!

We are all travelers as we pass over

the hills and valleys of life ...

But the journey of a thousand miles

STILL begins with

JUST

ONE

STEP ...

As did your journey through Phonics Pathways.

So where will you go now?

And what will you do?

It's a choice that's entirely up to YOU!

But wherever you go

and whatever you do ...

"This above all:

To thine own self

Be true!"

—William Shakespeare

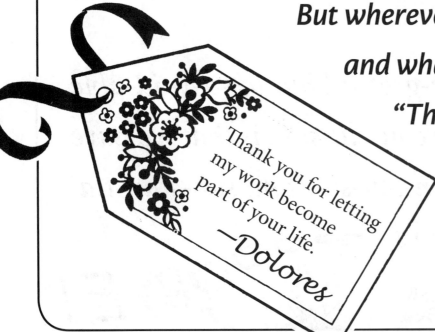

Thank you for letting
my work become
part of your life.
—*Dolores*

Appendix A: Reference & Supplemental Practice
 Spelling Strategies

Initially *Phonics Pathways* can be treated as just an "exposure" experience that will sensitize your students to the logic of the English language, and show them that specific rules exist that determine exactly how words are spelled.

By the end of the book, it may be time to begin teaching spelling in earnest. Spelling and reading enhance one another in a synergistic fashion—accurate spelling promotes accurate reading, and vice versa. And it's certainly easier to remember one rule for many words than it is to learn how to spell each word individually! (It's also very handy as well as economical to have reading and spelling programs available together in just one book.)

Have one notebook with three divided sections in it for each student—one section for copywork, one for dictation, and one for "trouble words." Copywork is always the best way to begin spelling lessons. Proceed as follows:

1. Have students turn to the Copy section of their notebooks. Begin with the first spelling lesson in the book, the "/k/ = c-, k-" rule on page 53. Explain the rule, and have students read some of the words again. Have them copy from five to ten words.

2. Older students should copy the rule itself as a header on top of the page, but younger students probably will not be ready for this much writing activity just yet. Check the work, and have students correct errors.

3. Have students turn to the Dictation section of their workbooks. Review the rule orally, and dictate about five to ten words for them to write down. Check the work, and have students correct any errors by rewriting the word correctly three times.

4. Students should keep a log of any spelling mistakes that were made in the "Trouble Words" section of their notebooks. Always include these words in the next day's dictation and use them in a spelling test once a week as well.

5. The next day, see if *they* can tell *you* what the rule is. Offer whatever help is needed. Keep dictating words from that lesson until the students can write the words from dictation without error.

6. After a while, begin dictating phrases and sentences—not just words. If dictation is limited to word families alone, students may not be able to spell the word outside of context. Only when students spell words correctly in sentences can you be absolutely certain that the spelling rule has been truly and thoroughly integrated. This activity helps develop memory and concentration as well.

For variety, try spelling with tile manipulatives, with magnetic letters, on individual whiteboards, or on a chalkboard. Work only about 10 to 15 minutes at a time when writing. Little hands and fingers *do* get tired!

Index to Spelling Rules and Patterns

Spelling & Pronunciation Chart

Short Vowels

ă	ě	ǐ	ǒ	ǔ
a c<u>a</u>t al h<u>al</u>f augh l<u>augh</u>	e p<u>e</u>t a <u>a</u>ny ea d<u>ea</u>f ai ag<u>ai</u>n	i h<u>i</u>d y g<u>y</u>m ui b<u>ui</u>ld	o t<u>o</u>p a w<u>a</u>nt	u p<u>u</u>p oo fl<u>oo</u>d o w<u>o</u>n a w<u>a</u>s ou y<u>ou</u>ng

Long Vowels

ā	ē	ī	ō
a-e t<u>a</u>pe ey th<u>ey</u> ai r<u>ai</u>n ea st<u>ea</u>k ay s<u>ay</u> ei v<u>ei</u>l eigh <u>eigh</u>t	e-e P<u>e</u>te ie f<u>ie</u>ld e w<u>e</u> i mar<u>i</u>ne ea m<u>ea</u>t y funn<u>y</u> ee s<u>ee</u>d ei c<u>ei</u>ling	i-e p<u>i</u>ne ie p<u>ie</u> i k<u>i</u>nd y tr<u>y</u> uy b<u>uy</u> igh r<u>igh</u>t ui g<u>ui</u>de	o-e h<u>o</u>me oe t<u>oe</u> o t<u>o</u>ld ow r<u>ow</u> oa s<u>oa</u>p ough d<u>ough</u>

Long Vowels

o͞o = ū	yo͞o = ū	Schwa ə = ǔ
u-e J<u>u</u>ne ue bl<u>ue</u> oo m<u>oo</u>n ui fr<u>ui</u>t o d<u>o</u> ou s<u>ou</u>p ew n<u>ew</u> oe sh<u>oe</u> wo t<u>wo</u>	u-e p<u>u</u>re ew m<u>ew</u>	a sof<u>a</u> o gall<u>o</u>p e spok<u>e</u>n u foc<u>u</u>s i san<u>i</u>ty

Miscellaneous / Diphthongs

ô	o͝o	oi ou
aw s<u>aw</u> o d<u>o</u>g au h<u>au</u>l al s<u>al</u>t ough b<u>ough</u>t all t<u>all</u> augh t<u>augh</u>t alk w<u>alk</u>	oo l<u>oo</u>k u p<u>u</u>t oul c<u>oul</u>d	oi b<u>oi</u>l ou <u>ou</u>t oy t<u>oy</u> ow h<u>ow</u>

Spelling & Pronunciation Chart

Consonants

k			f	j	z
k kid	ke bake	x tax	f fat	j just	z zip
c cat	ic picnic	qu quiz	ff huff	ge page	s is
ck sick	ick picnicking	ch school	gh rough	dge fudge	zz fizz
			ph phone		se rose

Consonants

sh	th	s	l	ch
sh ship	th thin	s sat	l lap	ch chat
s sure	th this	ss fuss	ll bell	tch hatch
ti nation		c city	le noodle	
si mansion		ce race		

Consonants / -ng, -nk Endings

wh	zh	-ng	-nk
wh when	z azure	ing sing	ink sink
	s measure	ang sang	ank sank
	g beige	ong song	onk honk
		ung sung	unk hunk

r-Modified Vowels

är	ôr		ʉr	âr
ar art	or for	ore more	er her	are care
	ar warm	our pour	ir sir	air pair
	oor door	oar roar	ur turn	ear bear
			or work	ere there
			ear heard	eir their

Plural Spelling Chart

s

To make most words plural, just add "-s":

top	tops	duck	ducks	pet	pets
tent	tents	sock	socks	melt	melts
cake	cakes	pine	pines	bean	beans
date	dates	ride	rides	feed	feeds

es

For words ending in "-sh," "-ch," "-tch," "-zz," "-x," or "-ss," add "-es":

fish	fishes	inch	inches	batch	batches
fizz	fizzes	miss	misses	tax	taxes
pinch	pinches	kiss	kisses	ditch	ditches
hiss	hisses	itch	itches	rich	riches

es

For words ending in "-y," change "y" to "i" and then add "-es":

ruby	rubies	penny	pennies	baby	babies
pansy	pansies	party	parties	hurry	hurries
try	tries	fly	flies	cry	cries
fry	fries	sky	skies	dry	dries

es

For words ending in "-f," change "f" to "v" and then add "-es":

loaf	loaves	wolf	wolves	leaf	leaves
elf	elves	life	lives	shelf	shelves
wife	wives	thief	thieves	strife	strives

Suffix Spelling Chart

(See also page 115.)

When adding a suffix beginning with a vowel: if a word ends in "-y" preceded by a *consonant,* change "y" to "i" first. Exception: keep the "y" when adding "ing":

-y

try	tries	tried	trying
study	studies	studied	studying
fry	fries	fried	frying
bumpy	bumpier	bumpiest	rides

When a word ends in "-y" preceded by a *vowel,* most of the time just add the suffix:

-y

play	player	played	playing
employ	employer	employed	employing

When a word ends in "-ie," drop the final "e" when adding a suffix beginning with a vowel. Exception: *change* the "ie" to "y" when adding "-ing":

-ie

lie	lies	lied	lying
tie	ties	tied	tying
die	dies	died	dying

Usually a word is not changed at all when adding a suffix beginning with a *consonant:*

dry	dryness	tie	tieless
use	useful	care	careful
bone	boneless	home	homeless

Student Achievement Chart

Name _____ Age _____ Grade _____

Phone _____ E-mail _____

Skill Level in *Phonics Pathways*	Review Page	Date Begun	Date Completed
Short vowels through review	16		
Two-letter blends through review	37		
Three-letter, short-vowel words through review	48		
"c-" and "k-" beginnings and "-ck" endings through review	57		
Double-consonant endings through review	69		
"-y" endings through review	73		
"-sh" and "-th" endings through review	79		
"-ch" and "-tch" endings through review	81		
"-ng" and "-nk" endings through review	86, 89		
Long "a" words (silent "e" ending) through review	92		
Long "i" words (silent "e" ending) through review	94		
Long "o" words (silent "e" ending) through review	96		
Long "u" words (silent "e" ending) through review	98		
Long "e" words through review	102		
All long-vowel words through review	105		
Short-vowel suffixes through review	113		
Short- and long-vowel suffixes through review	116		
Multisyllable words through review	117		
Consonant digraph beginnings through review	132		
Double-consonant beginnings through review	133		
r-modified vowel words through review	158		
Long-vowel digraph words through review	172		
Vowel diphthong words through review	180		
"/j/ = ge, gi, gy, -dge" words through review	183		
"-y, -ie" and "-f = -ves" words through review	187		
"/ŏŏ/ = oo, ou, u" words through review	190		
"/ô/ = au, aw, al, all, o" words through review	194		
Three-consonant beginning words through review	198		
Short-vowel spelling patterns through review	205		

Student Progress Notes

Name _____ Phone _____

Date	Page	Tutor Notes	(Special help, extra review, recommendations, etc.)	Tutor

Vision and Motor Coordination Training Exercises*

These exercises are designed to improve eye-hand-body coordination. Some experts feel they develop eye-tracking ability in particular. Not all children will be able to do all of these exercises. Try working through them, and see if you can come up with a small group of them that you both enjoy. It is important to practice them on a regular basis for maximum effectiveness, but feel free to vary them if a change is needed:

1. Have them hold their heads still, and follow with their eyes as you slowly move a small object (penny, head of a pencil, etc.) from far left to far right at eye level, back and forth several times. Now move it up and down, and diagonally. Then slowly bring the pencil in towards their noses while they focus as long as they can, and out as far as you can reach. Always move very slowly and smoothly.

2. Make a beanbag about 5 inches square (birdseed makes *wonderful* filling!) and throw it back and forth to them. (Beanbags are easy to catch and don't roll away when dropped.) Aim for a faster throw and catch. (They may wish to change to a ball when this skill is well developed.)

3. Have them lie on the ground, and tell them to raise their left legs, right legs, left arms, or right arms. After they can raise the correct leg or arm easily, have them try a combination of two together: "Left leg, right arm," etc.

4. While they are on the ground, tell them to make "angels in the snow": to move their arms and legs up and down against the ground. Then name a particular arm or leg, as in exercise 3. When they get proficient, have them combine an arm with a leg upon command, as in exercise 3.

5. Have them walk on a balance board (holding their hands if necessary), or some variation of it. If this is too difficult, have them walk all along a rope that has been laid across the floor, one foot in front of the other.

6. Have them march to an even beat, throwing opposite arms and legs forward, while you clap or beat a drum. Now have them clap and march at the same time.

7. See if they can crawl. If they cannot, have them practice crawling.

8. If a trampoline is available, have them jump on a trampoline. Hold their hands for safety!

9. If they are well coordinated, have them practice skipping.

10. Suspend a whiffle ball (plastic ball with cutouts) from the ceiling or rafter, about chest level. Have them "box" with alternate fists, aiming for a smooth, even stroke. Then have them hit the ball repeatedly with a paddle or a bat, trying to move it in the same direction as much as possible.

*No special claims are made for these exercises other than that they have been helpful to some students, including the author's own children. You may wish to check with your doctor before proceeding.

11. Suspend a whiffle ball at foot level, slightly off the floor. Have them kick with alternate feet, aiming for a smooth, even kick, sending the ball in the same direction each time. After a while, as they kick with their left feet, have them move their right arms slightly forward, and their left arms slightly back, alternating arms with legs.

The Following Exercises Help Develop Manual Dexterity:

12. Have them make large circles with both hands at the same time (chalk on blackboard or fingers on wall). Then reverse the direction. Now have them cross their hands over and *repeat* this exercise, if they can. This may be too difficult for many children, but is very useful if it can be managed.

13. Have each student crumple up a sheet of paper into a small ball, using only one hand. Then repeat this with the other hand. (Tissue paper is easiest; also try newspaper and writing paper.)

14. Sandpaper *greatly* increases the tactile experience! Cut out 3- to 6-inch letters from sandpaper, and glue them onto cardboard. Have them feel each letter with their fingers as they name the letter sound. Then have them trace it with their fingertip, and say the sound again.

15. To increase the kinesthetic experience, tell them to trace *big* letters with their fingertips on the wall (or with chalk on the blackboard, if available).

16. Tracing is *great!* Try tracing paper, and have them trace some of their favorite pictures with pencils. Later on have them trace large letters, and then progressively smaller ones. Always make sure they begin at the correct point and move their pencils in the correct direction.

17. Have them draw the following, using one continuous motion when possible:

Pyramid

(See also page 52.)

Practice these words until you are able to read them smoothly—each block of words has the same short-vowel sound. This part of *Pyramid* will help you blend letters into words (as will the exercises on page 40). (If you *do* find this kind of reading practice helpful, there is a whole book of pyramids available from Dorbooks.)

Next, read the *Pyramid* on the next page, which comprises the same words. This part of *Pyramid* will help you build words into sentences. Your eye tracking will *strengthen,* and your eye span will *lengthen!*

> The road UPHILL and the road DOWNHILL are the SAME ONE!

a	c-a	ca	ca-t	cat	
a	f-a	fa	fa-t	fat	
a	h-a	ha	ha-d	had	
a	b-a	ba	ba-g	bag	
a	a-n	an	an-d	and	
i	i-n	in			
i	h-i	hi	hi-d	hid	
i	b-i	bi	bi-g	big	
i	f-i	fi	fi-g	fig	figs
o	B-o	Bo	Bo-b	Bob	
u	g-u	gu	gu-m	gum	
u	n-u	nu	nu-t	nut	nuts

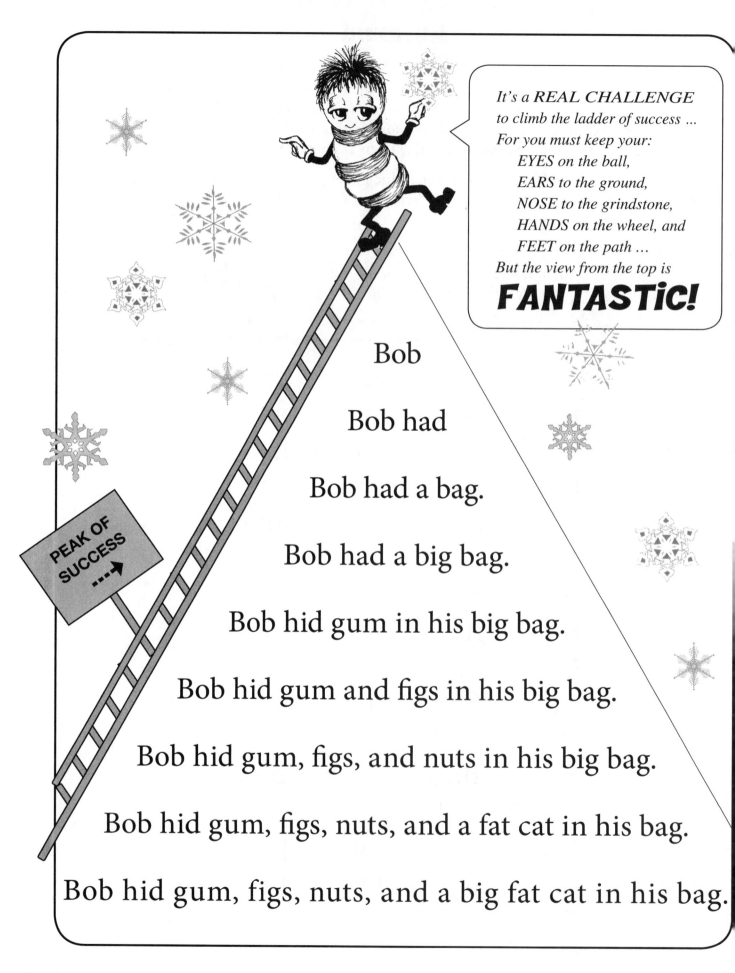

It's a **REAL CHALLENGE**
to climb the ladder of success ...
For you must keep your:
    EYES on the ball,
    EARS to the ground,
    NOSE to the grindstone,
    HANDS on the wheel, and
    FEET on the path ...
But the view from the top is
FANTASTiC!

PEAK OF SUCCESS

Bob

Bob had

Bob had a bag.

Bob had a big bag.

Bob hid gum in his big bag.

Bob hid gum and figs in his big bag.

Bob hid gum, figs, and nuts in his big bag.

Bob hid gum, figs, nuts, and a fat cat in his bag.

Bob hid gum, figs, nuts, and a big fat cat in his bag.

Appendix B: Games and Activities

HOT TIPS

1. *Echo* (for short-vowel sounds): Make a list of about ten words that *begin* with the short-vowel sound you are working on, such as the /ă/ in "apple," using the picture words from page 11 (the /ă/ page). Sprinkle in about five words that do not begin with that sound, such as "rug," etc.

   Mix the words up, and read them slowly with emphasis. Students should repeat the word if you say a word beginning with that sound, but put their hands over their mouths and say nothing if the word begins with *another* sound. Repeat this activity with the rest of the vowels as they are learned.

2. *All in a Row* (for short-vowel words): Have five students stand in a row in front of the class, each one holding up a sheet of paper with a very large vowel written on it. Read words containing random short-vowel sounds, each time choosing a student to go up and stand by the person holding the correct vowel and say the vowel sound. (For individuals, tack a poster of each sound to the wall and have your learner walk to the correct poster, stand by it, and say the sound. Also see numbers 3 and #4 on pages 4 and 5.)

3. *You're on the Air*: Everyone opens his book and reads the same page aloud. Walk around with a portable microphone, and choose one student to read into the microphone. All students should follow along silently while this student is reading aloud, and run their fingers under the word/sentence being read. Each one must be ready to be "on the air," as nobody knows who'll be chosen next!

4. *Fishing Marathon*: Copy the page you are working on and cut the words into equal sizes. Fold the words in half and put them in an empty tissue box. Divide the class into two groups. Students take turns reaching in the box, catching a "fish," and reading it. The first group to finish wins the fishing marathon!

5. *Lifeboat*: Put eight "lifeboats" (carpet squares, towels, etc.) on the floor in a row. Eight students march around them while you read a variety of words, most of which contain the sound you are working on, but some of which do not. When you read a word *not* having that sound, each student must sit on or touch a lifeboat. Remove one lifeboat each time. Students must share the dwindling supply until only one lifeboat is left. (Make sure it is the biggest one!)

6. *Musical Chairs*: Put seven chairs in a row, every other one facing backward. Eight students circle the chairs while you read a variety of words, most of which contain the sound you are working on, but some of which do not. When you read a word *not* having that sound, the students scramble to sit down. The student left standing goes back to his or her seat. Remove a chair and keep playing until only one student is left.

7. *Treasure Hunt*: Copy the page you are working on; cut the words, phrases, or sentences into equal sizes; and fold them up. Hide them around the room, and see who can find the most "treasures"! They must read each note as it is found. (Have a little treat folded up in some of them to make it more enticing!)

The Short Sheet of Vowels (See page 5.)   Name _____

Aa	Ee	Ii	Oo	Uu

The Shoo-Fly Shuffle

This is really another version of the *Short-Vowel Shuffle* (see page 5 for complete directions), but we can't call it that now because this game will be used with syllables and words from this point on, and not short-vowel sounds.

Let's call it the *"Shoo-Fly Shuffle."* In fact, *Shoo-Fly* actually was a Civil War nonsense song once. Originally it was kind of a shuffling dance, so that's a good name for it, because shuffling around your desk is one way to play it that is a lot of fun!

("Shoo-fly" can mean other things as well, such as a pie filled with molasses and brown sugar.) (*Mmmmmmmm …*)

See page 20 for vowels and complete instructions. This game can be especially helpful in developing blending skills all the way from two-letter syllables to multisyllable words:

Blendit! (Similar to *Bingo*)

See page 16 for complete directions. *Blendit!* can be played with two, three, or four players. Good readers can be paired with beginners because everyone has an equal chance of winning. *Everyone* loves to play *Bingo!* (And it's certainly a great way to reinforce learning …)

StarSearch

See page 37 for complete directions and page 38 for a sample game. It's always lots of fun to go "stargazing"! The one who finds the most star cards is the winner. (Or, for a real challenge, try counting the number of *stars* and see who has the most!)

Bag the Bugs

Complete instructions are on page 48, and a sample game is shown on page 49. It can be played by a single player, or with small-to-medium groups if you make up sufficient cards. (This game is always a favorite—students *love* the yucky bugs!)

Reviews and Results for the Classroom (Including ESL)

"Our school serves a diverse socio-economic population, with many students in the free and reduced lunch program, living in subsidized housing, and coming to school totally unprepared to learn. We established an in-school tutoring program with *Phonics Pathways*, using parent and community volunteers. First- to third-grade nonreaders were tutored fifteen minutes a day, three days a week.

"In less than a year test results showed the school advanced from having the lowest to the highest reading scores in the entire school district. Our teachers are elated! Fourth-grade teacher Pam Mendonca now has all of these 'graduates' in her class for the first time, and she observed: '*This is the most literate class I have ever had. Our tutorial program is worth its weight in gold!*' "

—Joe Madeiros, principal, Joe Mitchell School, Livermore, CA

"After only four months of using *Phonics Pathways* 100% of my bilingual Title One first-graders are reading the regular first-grade books. All of them have some level of limited English-speaking ability and come from poor economic standings. One-third of my students have one or more parents serving time in prisons. They now have the strategies they need to read. The best part is the match to Spanish phonics—it follows the same sound patterns. Now my parent helpers are using it at home, and my colleagues are all using it as well. I've had great success creating a balanced reading program for my students using your materials along with our district program. Thank you for creating such an effective program for everyone—teachers, parents, and most of all for *students!*"

—Tracy Ciambrone, M.A., bilingual first-grade teacher, San Jacinto, CA

"I have used *Phonics Pathways* as an excellent source of systematic phonics materials and ideas. It is yards ahead of available phonic workbooks and much more fun and interesting. It does not insult the student with "giveaway pages" that lead to quick answers with little understanding or learning. The introduction, reading manual description, and hints are excellent. I especially liked the reading sentences, which take so long to make up on your own. Kids desperately want to be able to read, and phonics taught in such an interesting, systematic way gives them some success right away. Excitement soon replaces their fear and discouragement, and they're off to the races!"

—Diane Ransford, teacher and tutor, Orinda, CA

"As a classroom teacher, I have found a real need in our reading curricula for good, consistent phonics. Children need a solid, sequential program which builds upon previously learned skills with small, incremental steps toward the whole. Your program offers just the right degree in advances to ensure success. I have found that frustration is almost entirely eliminated with your books. *Phonics Pathways* provides a solid base from which to teach the basic sounds that make up our language. From a teacher's perspective, the little proverbs scattered throughout the book offer great insight and encouragement. I have found my students understand and appreciate them much more than expected."

—Susan Ebbers, second-grade teacher, Livermore, CA

"Cristal, a Spanish girl in my second-grade class, could not read. Then I discovered your wonderful book. After three weeks she is progressing nicely with its orderly, step-by-step approach, and is delighted by the encouraging sayings and quotes. Her face just beams when I tell her *she* is the one climbing the oak tree to the top. Cristal is a different child! Thanks for turning the lights on for so many."

—Diane Sambrink, teacher, Raleigh, NC

"The administration of Cesar E. Chavez Middle School and I thank you for *Phonics Pathways*. I have been using your phonics program for the past one and one-half years in my Learning Handicapped Special Day Class, with gratifying results. The students are delighted! Allow me to wish you continued success with your publishing endeavors."

—John Milton, teacher, Hayward, CA

"*Phonics Pathways* takes all the guesswork and example-finding out of teaching reading. Each lesson is clearly laid out and accompanied by abundant examples that reinforce the point to be learned. Best of all, it is a complete program which meets the needs of *all* reading levels, from beginning to remedial.

"I use this book to complement and supplement the current school programs, which are so rich in literature. I really feel that I have finally found a winning combination that will provide students with the skill they need most of all in order to succeed—the skill of literacy. *Phonics Pathways* truly is a one-stop shopping dream!"

—Chris Cova, teacher and tutor, Folsom, CA

Reviews and Results for the Home-School

"I'm a new homeschooling Mom and was having tremendous success teaching my 8th grader with *Phonics Pathways,* but not until this month did I realize just how *much* success. He has been wearing glasses since 3rd grade—he had a muscle problem with astigmatism. We started with the book eight months ago, ten minutes a day. He had an eye exam last week, and now has 20/20 vision and is free from glasses—thanks to your eyerobics! I cannot thank you enough for your incredible book."

—Wendi Cody Hill, Morgan Hill, CA

"This is an intensive and incremental approach to teaching reading. It can be used with any age, beginning or remedial. Older students would not find this manual insulting or babyish. I especially liked the large, easy-to-read typeface, and each page is visually interesting and uncluttered. If you want a no-frills approach to phonics that almost teaches itself, this book is certainly worth considering."

—Mary Pride, *Practical Homeschooling*

"*Phonics Pathways* is a complete program. Teaching instruction on each page is brief enough so that no preparation time is needed. Each new concept taught is followed by words, phrases and sentences for practice, so no other reading material is necessary. Because of quick movement into blending practice, children are reading three-letter words very soon. Reading practice is designed to improve left-to-right tracking skills, especially important for preventing dyslexic problems. *Phonics Pathways* is very reasonably priced for such a complete program."

—Cathy Duffy, author, *Christian Home Educators Curriculum Manual*

"I have been using *Phonics Pathways* for approximately two years to teach my twins (now seven) how to read. I can't say enough good things about the program, and want to thank you profusely for developing it. This program has made such a difference in our family that I have continually recommended it. I used to work tutoring learning-disabled at a local community college, and they have ordered it on my recommendation."

—Kathleen Smith, Chico, CA

"We are home-schooling, and our nine- and seven-year-olds were convinced they would never read. We had spent well over $600 buying products to help our children learn, but would have been better off never to have bought a single one. Then I discovered *Phonics Pathways* in our local library. Now, only six months later, our older child reads anything he wants, and his sister is not far behind. We are absolutely thrilled with their progress and your book!"

—The Walter R. Wright family, Gnadenhutten, OH

"I never thought I would have to teach my children how to read at home. But by Christmas, my first-grader was coming home in tears saying that he was stupid since he couldn't read. Then I found your book. I knew exactly what to do and how to do it at each point, because each page has such clear directions. Your technique of putting new reading words in front of a sentence is just great. We spent only ten minutes a day working and ten months after we started he was a strong and successful reader with excellent comprehension. Best of all, his younger five-year-old brother learned along with him, and is now able to read simple books all by himself. *Phonics Pathways* has been a great success with my children. Please accept a heart-felt thank you!"

—Tasia James, Livermore, CA

"Using your book is one of the most exciting and gratifying experiences I've had as a parent. I'm so amazed at what our three-and-a-half year old is learning. She really enjoys Dewey the Bookworm, who makes each lesson such fun. Your program has empowered me to be able to do something I've always wanted to do but never knew how. I'm just thrilled with this program!"

—Julie Daly

"We are home-schooling and used what we thought to be 'good' phonics programs with our children, but all we achieved was frustration. Our older children did not begin reading until age nine. I had made a wish-list along the way of what I would like to see in a good phonics program. Naturally, it would be *user-friendly*—even for the Mom who had never taught phonics before. It would have a *minimum of sight words* which would be slowly introduced. Of course it would be *complete,* with separate readers not required. Most of all, *encouragement* for the teacher and student would continue throughout the lessons.

"*Phonics Pathways* is all of the above—plus more! Your explanation of dyslexia is simple and to the point. Our daughter has gone weekly to a Developmental Ophthalmologist, and the vision and motor coordination training exercises you have included in your book are the same exercises that she has done at home and in therapy. She is now improving by leaps and bounds. Thank you for offering to parents a very insightful phonics program."

—Jill Denly, Creative Home Teaching, San Diego, CA

Reviews and Results for Tutoring (Remedial, Special Ed, ESL, Adult)

"In the heart of Silicon Valley live a number of students from non-English speaking families of all cultures who cannot read. A state-of-the-art YES Reading Center was set up at Belle Haven School using *Phonics Pathways*, resulting in significant improvement of reading scores. There are now over fifty dedicated tutors, and Stanford University has donated a portable building and various furnishings to house this program. The teaching materials and dedicated volunteers are rendering rave results from teachers and parents!"

—Mary Shaw, board member, YES Reading Project, Menlo Park, CA

"*Phonics Pathways* has helped me immensely as an Orton-Gillingham tutor. It is both logically presented and easy to consult. Perhaps most importantly for dyslexic students, the pages of your book do not tend to strain students' eyes as do a number of other phonics books due to print size, style, or overcrowding. Students smile at 'Dewey the Bookworm' and his positive comments as they progress through your exercises. I will do my best to wear this book out, as well as share it with others who tutor."

—Roberta Puckett, Orton tutor, Schofield, WI

"I am a Special Education Speech Technician, and have found *Phonics Pathways* to be a wonderful resource to use for reading and spelling lessons as well as with our Speech Therapy and ESL students. I like the fact that we can combine and reinforce so many programs through one easy-to-use publication. The word lists give many good examples of targeted sounds. The sample sentences are great for speech students who need to listen for correct pronunciations. We are still in the early stages of discovering all of its uses and applications, but I want to thank you for your excellent reading program."

—Danna Johnson, speech technician, Palisades School District, Palisades, WA

"I am currently serving as a volunteer tutor for adult literacy in the Salt Lake group, 'Literacy Volunteers of America.' For the past three months I have used *Phonics Pathways* in my classes. I have to tell you, the lessons you provide are marvelous and work very well with adults who are learning the basic reading skills. Thanks for your hard work in writing it—you have served more people than you know, and have made a major contribution to many people's lives!"

—Cynthia Skousen, adult literacy volunteer, Salt Lake City, UT

"Our 3rd-grader's teacher told us he could not read. I got *Phonics Pathways* from the library, and in only four months Daniel was one of the best readers in his class! Also, he was just chosen 'student of the month.' As we worked with this book, I found I was also learning myself. This book should be obligatory reading for all first and second graders. Congratulations on writing a superb piece we so desperately need."

—Richard M. Low, M.D., president, Infor*Med Medical Information Systems, Encino, CA

"After my mom had a stroke she had trouble getting words from her brain to her mouth. Soon after she was back home I began using *Phonics Pathways* with her—she loved it! The sounds were one of the problem areas she had, and it helped her so much. She is writing out her own Christmas cards and reading 'baby' books now. Today I'm proud to say that our library has its own copy of this book. We also have a growing population of Mexican families in our area, and I notice that many Hispanic children are using it to learn English."

—Barb Tessmann, librarian, Oconom Public Library, Oconomowoc, WI

"When parents ask us what they can do to help their children read, we always recommend *Phonics Pathways*. It is easy to use and engaging for children. We find that many children need to learn to track left to right with their eyes, and find patterns and similarities among words. These exercises provide that kind of practice. We use this book, and can heartily recommend it."

—Joanne Abey, director, Tutorage Learning Center, Livermore, CA

"Our Ruth is hearing impaired, and has a cochlear implant which enables her to hear at about 30 decibels. Her ability to sound out words is limited, and until now she has made little progress in reading. The average reading level of deaf people in America is 4th grade, and we're deeply concerned about her reading. Your book now makes it easier, simpler, and more likely to succeed—we are systematically re-teaching all the phonics sounds. *Phonics Pathways* makes it a less anxious, more organized and 'do-able' task. We're with you in believing that even deaf students need a phonics base to break the barriers and become avid readers."

—Mary Lou Powell, Las Cruces, NM

About the Author

Dolores has been involved with education most of her adult life, ever since teaching her own children how to read. She has tutored reading for over thirty years, and collected classic old reading and spelling books from English-speaking countries all over the world. During this time she developed a unique teaching method that prevents or corrects reversals, which is similar in effect to exercises frequently prescribed by specialists to treat dyslexia. Finally, she organized and simplified all this information into one comprehensive reading and spelling manual—the award-winning and best-selling *Phonics Pathways.*

Phonics Pathways is now being used by parents and professionals worldwide, and has recently won its fifth national first-place award as "Best Phonics Program in the Country."

Starbucks and Hewlett-Packard have made a video clip of students using *Phonics Pathways* at the highly-successful YES Reading Center in Palo Alto (www.yesreading.org). This promotional video clip encourages volunteerism and was shown on every United Airlines flight in the country.

Dolores continues to write new material; set up school and community tutoring programs; and write articles for professional journals, such as *The California Reader* (California Reading Association), *Education Matters* (Association of American Educators), *The National Right to Read Report* (www.nrrf.org), and many others. She also writes and publishes a free ongoing, e-mail newsletter, *Phonics Talk* (www.dorbooks.com).

Dolores has received many honors and citations for her contributions to education, and she is listed in a number of *Marquis Who's Who* directories, including *Who's Who in American Women, Who's Who in the West, Who's Who in Education, Who's Who in America,* and *Marquis Who's Who in the World.*

Professional memberships include the Orton Dyslexia Society, California Association of Resource Specialists, Learning Disabilities Association, Association of American Educators, California Reading Association, Association of Educational Therapists, National Right to Read Foundation, Publishers Marketing Association, Bay Area Independent Publishers Association, and the Commonwealth Club of California.

Dolores lives with her husband, John, in the San Francisco Bay Area. They love to read, travel, and hike, and they have been known to go to any length to see a good play or movie. Most of all, however, they love to visit with friends and family. They have two beloved children and two adored grandchildren, whom Dolores also has taught how to read. She loves to paint with watercolors as well—if and when she can ever find time to do so!

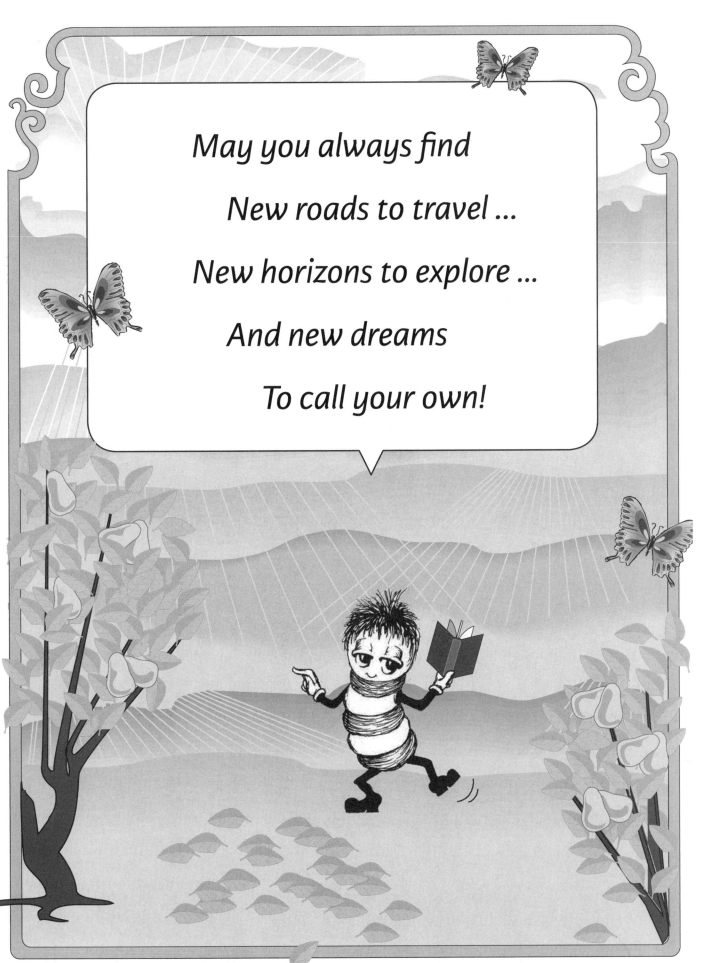

May you always find

New roads to travel ...

New horizons to explore ...

And new dreams

To call your own!